Pointing at the Moon

Teaching Martial Arts to Change Lives

Pointing at the Moon

Teaching Martial Arts to Change Lives

by
Neal Dunnigan

 Global Thinking Books

Copyright:

Published by:

Marketplace for a World
of Digital Content

Lulu Enterprises, Inc.
Morrisville, NC 27560

While every precaution has been taken in the preparation of this book, the publisher assumes no responsibilities for errors or omissions, or for damages resulting from the use of information contained herein.

Dedicated to:

Kenji Fujiwara Shihan (Master Teacher)

Tournament champion, teacher, leader, martial arts missionary, friend and mentor for many. His daily life exemplifies the contemporary martial way in a fashion that transcends cultural and stylistic differences. He is truly a teacher who helps change lives. Many thanks for his help and encouragement on this project.

Table of Contents

Preface

It is a good practice for martial arts teachers to keep a training notebook; not just a diary of training sessions and techniques, but also a workbook of challenges faced, insights gained, and lessons learned. I have given a great deal of thought to journaling my own training and teaching awakenings.

Eventually I came to the conclusion that organizing my thoughts would help me to better discipline my mind and guide my progress as a martial artist, even if this meant that I was doing some of my journaling retroactively.

I later decided that those same structured thoughts would allow me to be a better teacher; the journal would help me better communicate with and coach my students.

Eventually, I determined that presenting my musings in the format of this book would provide a tool for my students. Perhaps some of my students and colleagues can go a little further themselves by reacting to the thoughts that I have collected here.

The reader might find some great thoughts in this book. I did not originate them, I simply passed them on. In my prior book, *Zen Stories of the Samurai* (Global Thinking Books, 2004), I listed an extensive bibliography. I still recommend those readings to any serious student of the martial arts. This book does use a number of quotes from those sources. I wanted to tie my contemporary analysis to these classical sources so that a reader who was unfamiliar with them might be encouraged to go back and study the original sources.

This book did not come from a social vacuum. I spent many years discussing these concepts and ideas with martial arts colleagues. I also reached out to many colleagues outside of the martial arts world such as colleagues who have been long time sports coaches. I appreciate all of the knowledge that they have generously shared with me.

My own martial arts background is primarily in Japanese style martial arts and primarily Aikido. However, I did not write this as an Aikido book or Japanese martial arts book. I have tried to make the core of the book martial arts style agnostic. Some of my examples and terminology may be Japanese or Aikido oriented. That was my choice, in order to add more consistency to the text and this allowed me to speak from an area where I could be more authoritative. However, I think that slight cultural bias should not distract a reader from another martial arts style, or even a non martial artist from understanding the core messages of the book.

Keep in mind that is not the intent of this book to educate the reader in the specifics of the oriental cultures that formed the original world-view context for many of today's martial arts. Rather, this book is an attempt to identify a few of those key principles that are common across cultures and express them in a contemporary American context so that the reader can more directly evaluate their relevance.

In any event, I hope that this book will be another stepping stone for martial arts adherents, particularly those who might aspire to be teachers. The reader should remember that the thoughts that I have expressed should not be taken as absolutes. They are merely sign posts pointing both to the past and the future.

Introduction

When people study the martial arts, they may be surprised to find themselves in a teaching role very early on in their studies. For example, even a very junior student might be called upon by the martial arts teacher in this way:

- _Show_ the new person where the dressing room is.
- _Show_ the new person _how_ to tie their uniform.

This _showing how_ is the most fundamental mode of teaching in the martial arts. Senior students almost universally begin helping junior students on a one-to-one basis. This type of teaching role continues throughout one's martial arts studies as long as there are more junior students around to _show how_ things are done.

Later on, as the student advances, they may be called on to extend their _showing how_ from a one-to-one basis to a one-to-many basis. For example:

- _Go lead the warm-up exercises._
- _Get up and demonstrate this technique._

Still later on a student may be asked to fill in for the martial arts teacher as a substitute instructor in a special circumstance. For example:

- _Lead the Thursday class next week while I am away on vacation._

Finally a student may reach a point where they can substitute on a regular basis as an assistant instructor. For example:

- _Starting next week, you will begin teaching the Tuesday evening beginner's class._

The role of assistant instructor may reach a point where it includes programmatic and administrative responsibilities. For example:

- _Record the attendance at each class._
- _Beginning next month, you will be leading the Thursday evening children's program._

At various points along the way, a more senior student may be assigned some mentoring responsibilities for one or more junior students. Here the senior is not just passing information, but is charged with raising the junior students' level of skill. For example:

- *Walk through the testing criteria with the new student and get her ready for her upcoming test.*
- *Take the new student aside and review the basic kata with him.*

All of these steps show progressions:

> - *From working with an individual to conducting a class.*
> - *From teaching a skill to conducting an event to running a program.*
> - *From dispensing facts to mentoring progress.*

Showing how is typically a transfer of skills, communicated primarily through modeling and instruction. Some forms of martial arts don't require instruction methods any more sophisticated than this. For example, in tactical martial arts programs, students are not typically life-long martial arts learners and the martial arts teacher has only a limited duration of time to teach a fixed-length program. Likewise, any program focused primarily on beginners or children is, by its very nature, driven by the *showing how* mode of teaching.

There is a point in this evolution where teaching becomes very different. One way to describe it would be to say that, at this point, the teacher has started to not only *show how*, but also begins to *show why*. This *showing why* has two variations:

1. *Why does it work?*
2. *Why does it matter?*

The first question has a technical nature. Here the martial arts teacher needs to communicate an understanding of the technical science that underlies the martial art. Certainly martial arts theory without technique is not very useful. Conversely, technique without theory is inherently limited in it applications to the exact conditions under which the technique was initially learned. As the student progresses, the martial arts teacher is expected to take on a mode of monitoring and guiding a student's development over time. The martial arts teacher will need to perceive:

- *Where the student needs to make progress*
- *What habits or impediments has the student acquired*
- *What are the sequence of steps needed for the student to advance*

Depending on the style of martial arts and the personalities of the martial arts teacher and student, the approach can vary. In some situations, the martial arts teacher may take a more prescriptive approach to guiding the student. In other situations, the martial arts teacher may be more oblique and focus primarily on creating the training conditions for the student to self-discover their path to the next level. In either situation, the martial arts teacher's responsibilities remain the same.

When the martial arts teacher is instructing in the *show how* mode, the martial arts teacher may approach a student, interrupt them to make a correction, and then either model the correct form or apply body corrections to the student's own movements. However, when the martial arts teacher is in the *why does it work* mode, the martial arts teacher handles the situation differently. Here, when the martial arts teacher interrupts a student's practice to make a correction, the teacher may initiate a dialog something like this.

> Teacher – *"Do you remember what we said last week about positioning your feet when receiving this kind of attack?"*
>
> Student – *"Yes Sensei, you pointed out that we need to be off the line of attack."*
>
> Teacher – *"Good recall! Now let me see you apply that same principle to the new technique that we are doing right now."*

The second variation of the *show why* is more existential. This *why does it matter* question can also be expressed as *So what?*

In the olden days of martial arts, students would have a great deal of awe and even be somewhat intimidated by their martial arts teacher. In some earlier oriental cultures, the student would be very reluctant to even ask *why does it work*, let alone *why does it matter*. This is no so much the case in the contemporary culture of the Unites States. The martial arts teacher must always be ready to hear and deal with these kinds of questions. Of course, sometimes the answer might be to tell the student that they are not ready to understand the full answer. However, that answer must never be simply a convenient excuse for the martial arts teacher. The martial arts teacher must have sufficient understanding to address the question at a level that is comprehensible to the student.

This *why does it matter* question is the key connection to integrating martial arts to every day living. Consider this situation:

> Teacher – *"You are not turning your head enough before you do this block."*
>
> Student – *"Yes Sensei."*
>
> Teacher – *"Without turning your head, your field of vision will not be able to detect a change-up on you opponent's attack. This is a similar situation as when you cross the street. You*

would always need to look both ways before crossing the street. In this city, you are statistically more likely to be run over while crossing a street than you are to be attacked by an assailant using this particular kind of attack. It would be a foolish irony if you should allow yourself to be run over because you did not turn your head and see a car coming at you!"

The purpose of these scenarios is to dramatize that:

- *There is a progressive evolution in the modes of instruction applied by the martial arts teacher as the student becomes more advanced.*
- *As the martial arts practitioner moves to the higher modes, martial arts are more integrated into their everyday lives. The teacher's instruction and guidance must facilitate that process.*
- *The modes of teaching that martial arts instructors use have relevance to their own personal development as well as the students' development.*

From an historical perspective, it is easy to show the significance of integrating martial arts into daily lives of the martial arts practitioner. For example, nearly 400 years ago, the sword master Miyamoto Musashi reinforced this idea in his <u>Book of Five Rings</u> where he describes a list of attributes for people desiring to become his martial arts students:

...This is the Way (i.e., lifestyle) for those who want to learn my strategy (i.e., martial arts style):
- *Do not think dishonestly.*
- *The value of the Way is found in training.*
- *Become acquainted with every art.*
- *Know the Ways of all professions.*
- *Distinguish between gain and loss in worldly matters.*
- *Develop intuitive judgment and understanding for everything.*
- *Perceive those things which cannot be seen.*
- *Pay attention even to trifles.*
- *Do nothing which is of no use.*

Notice that the sword master did not tell his students that they needed to be fierce or brave or physically tough in order to be his students. His prerequisites for his students are all aimed at sharpening their discernment in both martial arts and every day matters. What is particularly interesting about Musashi's list was that it was created in a time when fighting with a sword had direct combat applications in everyday life.

Coming up to modern times, the following statements by the All Japan Kendo Federation (AJKF) capture the official aspirations of this modern martial art, with respect to its everyday influence on it practitioners:

The Concept of Kendo:

The concept of Kendo is to discipline the human character through the application of the principles of the Katana (sword).

The Purpose of Practicing Kendo is:

- *To mold the mind and body,*

- *To cultivate a vigorous spirit,*

- *And through correct and rigid training to strive for improvement in the art of Kendo,*

- *To hold in esteem human courtesy and honor,*

- *To associate with others with sincerity,*

- *And to forever pursue the cultivation of oneself.*

- *This will make one be able:*

  - *To love his/her country and society,*

  - *To contribute to the development of culture*

  - *And to promote peace and prosperity among all peoples.*

So as a martial arts student progresses, the lessons of martial arts training are expected to become more and more the lessons of everyday life. Martial arts become more holistic over time. Likewise as the martial arts student progresses, the martial arts teacher can more frequently apply the higher-level teaching modes. The following table summarizes how these interactions play out.

Levels of Martial Arts Teaching		Teaching Vs Life		
		Martial Arts Teaching Mode	Real-Life Analog	Real-Life Implications
⇧ Progression ⇧	Level 3	*Wisdom Based: "Why does it Matter?"*	*Larger World View*	*"I can apply what I learned in one discipline to other seemingly unrelated contexts."*
	Level 2	*Knowledge Based: "Why does it Work?"*	*Body of Knowledge*	*"I can mentally decompose skills that I have learned and apply the elements in new and different ways."*
	Level 1	*Skills Based: "Showing How"*	*Bag-of-tricks*	*"I only know what I was shown."*

Table 1: Progressive Modes of Martial arts teaching

The point being made here is a matter of abstract principle and therefore intensely subjective. An argument could be made that there are four or five levels, rather than three. It could be that some other points of view are more correct. It is also possible that there are multiple correct points of view depending on the context of one's observation. For purposes of illustration three teaching levels have been suggested here. However, this is simply a convenience for illustrating the point of a continuum of evolution. The main consideration is that there are levels and that they are progressive. These levels do not simply build on each other because they are not exclusive of each other. While a martial arts teacher may instruct a novice student with a 98% concentration at Level 1, it is likely that the martial arts teacher will still include some minimal amount of Level 2 content. The situation would be analogous with an advanced student. In that case the martial arts teacher might be able to spend more time at the higher levels, but the martial arts teacher would not eliminate the lower level completely when teaching.

One of the main considerations for martial arts teachers is that as the level of teaching advances, the integration of the martial arts into everyday life increases.

In industry, the martial arts term "black belt" has been borrowed by quality management advocates and applied to their Six-Sigma processes. Six-Sigma is a discipline for identifying and correcting dysfunctional and inefficient processes in industry. A person who understands and internalizes the techniques and principles of Six-Sigma to the point at which they are designated a "black belt" has reached the level at which:

- *Their ability to observe data, extract pertinent facts, perceive patterns, and understand cause and effect in industrial processes is fundamentally and permanently changed.*
- *They have reached a point where they can observe, analyze, and correct process problems in any setting, not just their own industry. Their learning is transferable.*

So why did the Six-Sigma advocates adopt the designation "black belt"? Perhaps it was simply a marketing device to imply that their experts were intellectually tough and they wanted to brand themselves as industrial top guns. Or perhaps it was the recognition that a martial artist is not just a technical expert, but a well rounded and well integrated individual.

This concept of well-roundedness was captured back in the later Japanese feudal period with this expression about the education of a samurai:

The pen and the sword in accord.

This expression meant that the "expert" in the martial arts was expected to maintain a balanced mastery of skills in all aspects of life. In this context, "accord" means more than a simple proportional allocation of training time. More significantly, it implies that study in one area complements and advances study in the other.

The sword master Miyamoto Musashi reinforced the idea in his <u>Book of Five Rings</u>:

> *There are various ways (i.e., way of life, vocations, avocations, professions). There is the way of salvation by the law of Buddha (i.e., clergy), the way of Confucius governing the Way of learning (i.e., educator / consultant / civil service), the way of healing as a doctor, as a poet (i.e., artist) teaching the way of the tea ceremony, archery, and many arts and skills. Each man*

*practices as he feels inclined. It is said the warrior's is
the twofold Way of pen and sword, and he should have
a taste for both Ways.*

In addition to being a totally dedicated martial artist, Miyamoto Musashi was
also renowned as an author, painter and sculptor. He clearly exemplified the
balance of "pen and sword" in his own life.

This life balance is something that the martial arts teacher has a duty to
convey to the student. To do this it is essential that martial arts teachers first
understand it themselves. Ideally, it is something that the martial arts teacher
should be living continuously.

Even in the contemporary common culture of the U.S. there is some
recognition of this idea as it relates to the martial arts.

In U.S. pop culture there is the representation of the bad martial arts teacher.
This is aptly depicted in the *Karate Kid* movie franchise where the antagonists
are short sighted, violent teachers representing the dark side of the martial
arts. There are also pop representations where the martial arts teacher is
portrayed as ineffectual and takes the role of comic relief, rather than that of
antagonist. This comic version is represented by the teacher of "Rex-Kwon-
Do" in the movie *Napoleon Dynamite* and by the "Ameridote" teacher in the
Internet video series *Enter the Dojo*. In these cases, the characterizations of
bad martial arts teachers are largely based on the lack of integration that they
demonstrate between their martial arts and everyday life.

The remainder of this book is a collection of essays about the art of teaching
martial arts. The book examines a number of topics. In each case the teaching
lesson has an implication for both the student and the teacher as well. In some
of the essays, the life lesson to the teacher is more clearly spelled out, in others
it is left for the reader to meditate upon and draw their own conclusions.

The essays in this book are arranged into three sections.

The first section, Frameworks of Understanding, has to do with organization
of thought. A martial arts teacher cannot properly present material which is
not well organized. Likewise people cannot progress through their lives
without some compass and a world view that provides a rational and
consistent context for the situations that they experience.

The second section, The Mind of the Teacher, deals with the matter of egos.
This is a critical issue in the teacher-student relationship. More importantly it
is a key issue for everyone's own personal development. Hopefully, by being
diligent in the teaching role, martial arts teachers can be successful in
overcoming their personal ego issues and help their students to do the same.

The third section, Extending it Forward, looks at the legacy a person creates when they accept the role of teacher. Human beings are mortal and everyone's impact on earth is very limited, even to the extent of being innocuous over time with respect to the universe. However, for those people with families, it is easy to see how they can, for good or bad, influence at least a generation or two of descendents.

For those who are teachers, there is the potential to go even further. As we will see as we progress in the book, martial arts teachers indeed have an inlfuence, which while not great from the universe's perspective, is still well beyond that of the average person. How does a martial arts teacher want to manage that responsibility? Are they willing to stand by it, and be accountable for it, in this world and possibly the next?

Section 1 – Frameworks of Understanding

> *...A commander's strategy, which requires him to make something large out of something small, is comparable to the making of a huge statue of Buddha from a foot-high scale model. I cannot write in detail how this is done. The principle of strategy is to know ten thousand things by learning one thing...*
>
> Book of Five Rings, Miyamoto Musashi

A martial arts teacher, like any teacher, must be organized. However, when it comes to teaching martial arts, it is not sufficient to simply be operationally organized. Certainly things like class schedules, lesson plans, examination criteria, and the mechanics of instruction are clearly necessary. However, this kind of operational organization is only a minimum starting point for teaching martial arts. At a more fundamental level, martial arts teachers must also have a high level of mastery over the relationships between all of the techniques in their arts. Martial arts teachers must understand:

- The relationships of the various techniques in their style as they relate to each other
- The relationships of the various techniques in their style as they relate to the general underlying principles
- The situational contexts behind the various techniques in their style
- How by appropriately applying those understandings, a martial artist can uncover different solutions to problems of a martial nature and the everyday problems of living

When all of those facets are brought together into an organized body of knowledge, the result is called a model. One example of a martial arts model is the one developed by the U.S. Marine Corps for their Marine Corps Martial Arts Program (MCMAP). The following figure depicts how MCMAP has attempted to organize the knowledge required for their martial arts practitioners and martial arts teachers.

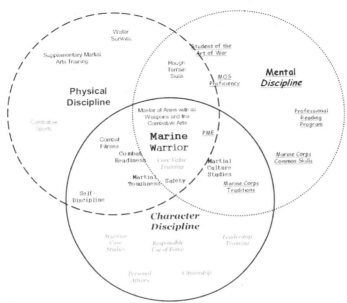

Figure 1: Marine Corps Martial Arts Program (MCMAP) Model

Notice that the MCMAP martial arts model:
- Includes many different aspects of the martial arts, both tactical and holistic
- Organizes the specific facets by domains and recognizes that a particular facet can be a participant in multiple overlapping domains

Even this superficial look at the MCMAP martial arts model illustrates the complexity inherent in creating a model of the martial arts.

Taking a step back from the specific MCMAP martial arts model, consider how a martial arts teacher from any martial arts style might try to organize their own thoughts about martial arts from their own individual perspective.

Mental models that martial arts teachers use to organize their knowledge of martial arts have both an applied aspect and a sustaining aspect.

The applied aspect refers to the application of a mental model to new situations. The mental model helps people dissect, discriminate, and associate what they perceive in relation to what they already know. When the martial arts teacher perceives something and recognizes it, the mental model helps the martial arts teacher to effectively deal with it. The mental model also is the basis for determining whether that which is being perceived is a new discovery or already known.

In the following simplified view of the martial arts teacher's brain, assume that there is a mental model of what the martial arts teacher knows about martial arts and martial arts teaching. The mental model is composed of three basic components:

- *Knowledge Base* – an accumulation of learned facts and experiences
- *Associations* – an index of connections associating the various elements in the knowledge base
- *Paradigms* – filters that determine how to interpret the information presented by a group of associations

The martial arts teacher's mental model must always be in a state of refinement. This is the sustaining aspect of a martial arts mental model. The frequent repetition of familiar situations or the occasional occurrence of significant familiar situations should cause the existing mental model to be optimized by streamlining and reinforcing existing *Associations* within the mental model and adding additional weight to content that is already in the *knowledge base.*

Unfamiliar information expands the mental model. If the mental model's current *associations* and *paradigms* can accommodate the new information, then the new information is incorporated into the mental model's *knowledge base.* When the new information does not "fit" the model, then the model needs to change. The metal model needs to adopt new *paradigms* to account for the new information. It is possible that the new *paradigms* might conflict with existing *paradigms,* in this case the existing *paradigms* need to be changed (i.e., corrected or abstracted and expanded) to coexist with the new *paradigm.* This results in an epiphany or a metamorphosis of the mental model.

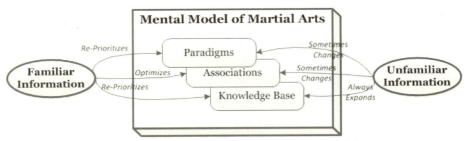

Figure 2: Mental Model for Understanding Martial Arts

Of course, people do not always take the path to greater wisdom. It is possible for individuals to neglect the development of their mental models. This is true in both martial arts teaching and life in general. People can choose to be lazy or resistant to knowledge. This might be a result of the fact that reorganizing the mental model *paradigms* can be stressful work. When exposed to new information, a person can simply disregard it. It can be put in the *knowledge base*, but classified as "unreliable" or "unproven". This removes the need to reorganize the *associations* or tamper with the existing *paradigms*. In psychology, terms like *repression, suppression,* and *transference* are used to describe the misclassification and mishandling of information by a mental model. In every day life, people use terms like denial and skepticism. Whatever terms describe it, it is dysfunctional and harmful to the development of a martial arts teacher.

A more figurative representation of this is captured in the Zen story of the student and the martial arts teacher.

> *A student approaches a famous martial arts teacher to ask for admission to his school. The teacher says, "Classes are over for today, but come on inside and join me for tea and we can discuss your application for admission." So the teacher and prospective student enter and sit down for tea. As they are having tea, the student is monopolizing the conversation and pontificating about various styles of martial arts that he had practiced and of the various theories about the martial arts that he had concocted. At some point the martial arts teacher notes that the prospective student's cup is empty and the martial arts teacher interrupts the student to ask the student if he would like more tea. The prospective student raises his cup for the teacher to fill. The teacher pours the tea into the prospective student's cup, fills it and then keeps on pouring. As the hot liquid overfills the cup and spills onto the prospective student's hand, he shouts, "Master, my cup is overflowing! It can not take in anymore tea!" The teacher stops pouring and responds, "Yes, you are correct, a full cup does not have room for more tea. Our minds are like teacups; when they are already filled completely with old ideas, it is not possible to make room for new ones. If you really want to be my student, you must first empty your mind."*

In that classic story, the lesson is directed at the student. However, for this discussion the lesson is that the martial arts teacher needs to be a perpetual student and always be able to respond appropriately to new information.

Take a hypothetical example of a martial arts teacher observing a new technique demonstration from some other martial arts style. Consider what different martial arts teachers might be thinking while they observe something that they have never seen or thought of before.

It is possible that the martial arts teacher's current mental model can absorb what they have witnessed without cognitive conflict. For example:

> *Yes. I see what just happened. That was wonderful. It was a different application of technique that applied*

principles that I was aware of in a new and productive
way. I'll make a mental note of this for the future.

It is also possible that the martial arts teacher's current mental model cannot absorb what they have witnessed without cognitive conflict. For example:

Yes. I see what just happened. That was wonderful. I
don't quite follow what just happened. Maybe I did not
understand the basics of my own style as well as I
should have or else I should have been able to integrate
what I saw into what I have already learned. I'll need to
go back and think about this to determine if I have
fundamentally missed something in my learning of my
style or if I need to expand my views on martial arts
theory.

It is also possible that the martial arts teacher's current mental model cannot absorb what they have witnessed without cognitive conflict and they choose to disregard it. For example:

Yes. I see what just happened. Who knows what those
people do. It would probably never work in the street.

It is worth noting that part of the impact of Zen Buddhist thinking on martial arts teaching is to challenge those *associations* and *paradigms* in the mental model. The Zen tradition recognizes the propensity to misclassify and mishandle information as the ego tries to preserve the status quo in the mental model. In the Zen tradition, the martial arts teacher assaults the mental model, not with new information aimed at the *knowledge base*, but with paradoxical scenarios that challenge the mental model's current *associations* and *paradigms*. The concept is that such challenges (e.g., pouring hot tea on the hand) break down the student's barriers to new ways of thinking.

To master the body of knowledge that is represented in a martial arts, teachers must apply a set of mental disciplines to organize their thoughts and enhance their mental model of martial arts. These methods can include all kinds of structures, including ontologies, taxonomies, patterns, models, etc. There are entire bodies of academic discipline related to this which are beyond the scope of this book. For purposes of this discussion, the term *frameworks* will be used to represent all of those mental structures.

It is not enough that martial arts teachers have frameworks to organize the knowledge of their martial art. A martial arts teacher must also be have frameworks that:

- Relate martial arts to everyday situations

- Accommodate the transmission of knowledge and proficiency from teacher to student
- Have the ability to dynamically adjust according to the context of the situation

A well know example of connecting martial arts to everyday life is the classic (16th century C.E.) <u>Book of Five Rings</u>. In that book, sword master Miyamoto Musashi uses the metaphor of carpentry to illustrate technique, lifestyle, and teaching principles of the martial art of fencing. The ability to associate freely between the martial arts and a very different discipline like carpentry shows that the author had a very integrated mental model of the martial arts.

This disciplined approach to thinking is a key lesson to be learned for any martial arts teacher. It would be very odd if a martial arts teacher would have a clear mental approach for applying and explaining the multifaceted applications of their art for combat, but not have a mental framework for understanding his or herself in relation to the everyday world around them.

This section of the book will explore some of the key areas where a martial arts instructor uses frameworks to establish a system of organized thought about a martial art and interaction of students and teachers.

Certainly martial arts teachers are not all of the same mind when it comes to how they think about teaching their arts. This is to be expected since they all come from different backgrounds, experiences, and traditions. So it is natural that instructors from different styles and backgrounds would express themselves differently. However, good martial arts teachers tend to have some common personal characteristics, such as:

- **Observing:** Noticing what is going on around during class, outside of class, at the school, and outside of the school.
- **Listening:** Paying attention to what the students and others are trying to communicate. Being an active listener and seeking to correctly understand others.
- **Explaining:** Communicating verbally to others in a respectful, organized, and effective way.
- **Modeling:** Communicating by actions that are consistent with the intent of the message and the core values behind it.

We would expect to see these characteristics carried over into the teacher's everyday life. Certainly, we would never expect all martial arts teachers to have the same professional interests, or common view on politics, religion, or philosophy. However, the ability to manage a mental framework capable of consuming a martial art indicates a general capacity to deal with large universal concepts. So we should expect to see in the daily life of a martial arts teacher the characteristics of being steady, connected, adaptable, and perceptive.

Martial Arts: What and Why?

A common subplot in the Japanese *chambara* genre of samurai movies involves a young warrior who tags along, eagerly observing the actions of one of the main protagonists. In this subplot, the young warrior is desperate to discover what it means to be a samurai. Of course, the young warrior is in fact usually already a samurai just by virtue of his social class. This subplot device uses the role of the young warrior to raise the question in the audience's minds:

What is the essential inner nature that defines the character of a true warrior?

Coming back from the chambara movies into current time and place, the same question can be asked about contemporary martial artists. Why would someone spend hundreds of hours each year training in the martial arts? Is there more to martial arts training than conditioning, katas, and sparring? Why would someone spend even more effort to teach martial arts? Is there some benchmark other than tournament trophies or black belt rankings that can measure the character of a true martial artist?

Before asking why someone would study, much less teach martial arts, it is worthwhile to reflect on what the term *martial arts* means in contemporary American English. A very basic definition, such as this one from Wiktionary begins to peel that onion.

Martial Arts:
Noun: 1. Commonly, any of several fighting styles which contain systematized methods of training for combat, both armed and unarmed; often practiced as a sport, e.g. boxing, karate, judo, Silat, wrestling, or Muay Thai
2. Military skills, proficiency in military strategy, prowess in warfare

Wiktionary

In this case, Wiktionary is a good starting point for a definition because it is a collaborative Wiki-based dictionary. Since the idea here is to understand what people commonly think about the definition of martial arts, a Wiki-based source is very appropriate.

Martial arts teachers must not only understand what they think about martial arts. Martial arts teachers must also understand what prospective students think about martial arts when they first enter the door of the martial arts school. Without this awareness, it will be difficult for the martial arts teacher to engage the new student effectively.

The definition describes martial arts as a collection of fighting systems. That is certainly true. The definition also makes important mention that martial arts training may be armed or unarmed and may also include an aspect of competitive sports. That is also correct. The problem with this particular definition is that it does not provide any insight or understanding into the intrinsic nature of martial arts. To advance an understanding of martial arts, it is necessary to look beyond a taxonomic-based definition to one that is focused more on martial arts from the practitioner's perspective.

Consider this description of martial arts, this time from another Wiki-based source, Wikipedia.

> *Martial Arts:*
> *The martial arts are codified systems and traditions of combat practices. They are practiced for a variety of reasons, including self-defense, competition, physical health and fitness, as well as mental, physical, and spiritual development.*

Wikipedia

This definition is less concerned with the taxonomy of the systems that compose martial arts. It also points out that martial arts have a combat origin and that they involve some systematic approach. It also begins to address the question of *why martial arts* and describes some of the perceived benefits of martial arts training.

Looking at the current state of American culture as it defines martial arts, it is expected that students now entering martial arts practice are most likely informed by the media; including:

- Movies
- Video games
- The Internet

In the case of contemporary movies, martial arts are idealized or romanticized (e.g., the *Karate Kid* movie franchise) or abstracted into a surreal representation (e.g., *Teenage Mutant Ninja Turtles* and *Kung Fu Panda* movie franchises).

In all of these contemporary cases, the media view of martial arts projects into the common culture, bringing some genuine elements of martial arts, but it also takes great liberties and compromises some intrinsic martial arts principles.

So, if the common view of martial arts in American popular culture is compromised by commercialism, how can a teacher relate the true meaning to the students? An even more important consideration is, how can martial arts teachers keep themselves on track in a culture whose pervasive media-based view of martial arts is self-serving and does not specifically align with the traditional martial art perspectives?

In our modern society, it is more efficacious to think of martial arts as disciplines that people choose to submit themselves to. This idea is grounded in the old concept of "a way of life" as captured in the Japanese word *do* or the Chinese word *tao*. Many martial art styles have names that end in the suffix *do*: Ju*do*, Tang Soo *Do*, Hapki*do*, Jeet Kune *Do*, Aiki*do*, Ken*do*, Kyu*do*, Taekwon*do*, etc. However, the concept of a discipline as a way of life is largely an academic abstraction in the mainstream of contemporary western culture.

There are some examples on the periphery of contemporary American society where this concept of a way of life still exists. Interestingly enough, many of these examples are religious in nature. Consider the lifestyle commitments of a Catholic nun in a religious order, or a member of an Old Order Amish community, or a practitioner of Haredi Judaism. These can be seen to be ways of life, similar in many ways to the term *do* as it is used in the term *budo* (i.e., *the martial way*) or in the older term *bushido* (i.e., *the way of the warrior*). Some of the noteworthy characteristics of these examples are:

- Lifelong commitment to a singular pursuit.
- A willingness to peacefully submit to the discipline of that lifestyle.
- Recognition that the commitment to the life style represents some separation from a substantial part of the rest of society.
- The avocation that is being followed defines the person's every-day life in terms of their goals, choices, priorities, and world view.
- A code of behavior that permeates the everyday aspects of their lifestyle, not just the portion related to their primary identification.

Unlike the religious examples cited above, the study of martial arts is not typically motivated by a belief in a higher power, but rather by an inner power. It is somewhat easier to justify and sustain a dedicated way of life when it is seen as a divine calling with extended benefits in some after life. Of course it is not possible to rationalize that with martial arts. The example of Olympic and other world-class athletes training to compete in non-commercial sports are examples of people driven hard by self-motivation. This was even acknowledged as far back as the 1st century C.E. when the Christian apostle, Paul, admonished his followers in ancient Corinth that even athletes competing for transient recognition (i.e., a laurel wreath) were showing more dedication than many religious people pursuing an eternal reward (I Corinthians 9:24-26).

Unlike past cultures of other places and earlier times, contemporary Americans are not born into anything related to martial arts. There is no externally enforced duty to train in martial arts. Nor is there a culturally encouraging support system of traditions that aids the pursuit of martial arts training. People are free to choose and change their interests in martial arts. Martial arts are truly elective pursuits for contemporary Americans.

However, whether one chooses to train for a short duration or their whole life, or whether one chooses to train more intensively or less intensively within the bounds of those parameters, one is still submitting themselves to the discipline of the martial arts. Consequently, although few people in today's society pursue martial arts as a way of life, all people who pursue martial arts are submitting to a certain discipline.

This idea of disciplined training is not unique to oriental martial arts cultures. A very western and pragmatic example of this point of view is captured in this succinct quote about military discipline attributed to Field Marshal Erwin Rommel:

"Sweat saves blood, blood saves lives, and brains save both."

Given those considerations, a different working definition of martial arts is being proposed for this book. The attempt is to expand on the previous definitions to include additional relevant factors that were just discussed. So as a working definition, for purposes of understanding martial arts in the context of this book, a general and broad contemporary definition of martial arts will be:

> *The martial arts are disciplines by which people train themselves, using both their physical and mental capabilities, to triumph in physical conflicts. These conflicts may be contrived as in sports competitions, they may be planned as in a tactical operation, or they may be extemporaneous as in self-defense. The physical and mortal natures of the conflict may be explicit or implicit. By engaging in this training, martial arts practitioners seek to advance their personal development and gain greater insight into every day situations, both martial and non-martial.*

Pointing at the Moon: Teaching Martial Arts to Change Lives

Certainly in such a broad definition of martial arts it is necessary to note that the emphasis of why people practice martial arts varies to some degree, not only according to the practitioner, but also according to the specific martial arts style and school. The following table is an illustration of this point. American society generally accepts the notion that sports and martial arts build character. However, because of the time-boxed nature of tactical martial arts training, it can be a bit of a stretch to expect very much character development. Likewise, sport and youth oriented programs will focus more within the constraints of fair play and less lethal simulation in their training.

Martial Art Style/ Program Orientation	Emphasis	
	Character Development	Life or Death Training Focus
• Traditional	High	High
• Sports	High	Low
• Youth	High	Low
• Tactical	Low	High

Table 2: Emphasis and Martial Art Styles

This section of the book addresses just one of the alternative definitions of martial arts. That particular definition is being used here to set the stage for the rest of the information in this book. However, martial arts teachers need to reflect within themselves and assess the specific meaning of martial arts that they want to use to guide them and their students.

An Evolution within an Evolution

Martial arts teachers are like riders on a moving passenger train. The riders can move from car to car, or go from side to side of the train, but at the same time, they are being carried forward by the train along the path of its tracks.

The movement of the rider within the passenger train is analogous to the way good martial arts teachers are always dynamically evolving their methods based on their interaction with the students in their class.

The speed and direction of the moving train as it travels along its tracks is analogous to the on-going changes in martial arts styles and society at large. As martial arts teachers evaluate and evolve their own teaching effectiveness, based on their interaction with their students, they also need to evolve their teaching based on larger externally driven changes.

Martial arts teachers need a way of setting direction while situations continually evolve, both with individual students and in the larger world.

A *perspective* is a framework that allows changing events to be understood in the context of some organized and trusted body of information. The ability to apply the proper perspective allows people to take an event and see it as meaningful rather than isolated. This process provides the basis for the most essential human sentient capabilities. These include understanding of cause and effect, prediction, self-awareness, and deductive/inductive reasoning.

In order for martial arts teachers to provide a sense of perspective to their students, the teachers must first have a sense of perspective themselves. It is safe to say, perspective is fundamental to higher level martial arts training. Knowing when to engage and when to withdraw from an adversary, understanding the larger situation around a confrontation, reading an opponent's intentions - these are all examples of instances where martial arts practitioners need to have a sense of perspective. Perspective is equally important in teaching martial arts as well.

The martial arts teacher must always have a perspective of the student's overall physical capabilities, their cognitive level of understanding, and their technical proficiency level. The martial arts teacher must have a perspective of these things both for each student individually and collectively for all of the students in a given training class. This sense of perspective gives the martial arts teacher a general understanding of the correct level of material to be presented based on composite understanding of the students' collective capabilities. This understanding helps martial arts teachers to set their teaching expectations and monitor their teaching results. Since most martial arts classes contain students with a range of experience and skills, it is not unusual to expect different results from different students in the same class. For example, within in the same class, a martial arts teacher might be concurrently seeking to achieve three results:

1. A needed review for most students
2. A breakthrough moment for a few students
3. A stretch objective for some students

Likewise, the martial arts teacher must have a perspective to judge the students' specific situation at any point in time.

For example, at different points during a class, have any of the students changed their levels of focus or their engagement in the training session? By observing the students over the course of a class, the martial arts teacher will have a perspective to detect if any of the students have become tired, distracted, injured, or confused. This allows the martial arts teacher to adjust the presentation of material to overcome or to otherwise mitigate any transient situational impediments to the learning process.

Martial arts teachers need a perspective of their martial arts styles' evolution over time. It may be possible that some martial arts styles might be narrow enough that they can still be taught the same way today as they were taught when they were originated. However, that situation would be a rare exception. The suggestion here is not that the core values and essence of martial art styles change, rather the idea is that the teaching methods will continually and gradually evolve. Typically, martial arts teachers need to have a perspective that allows them to see where their martial arts style has been and suggest to them where it is going over time.

To accomplish this understanding, there are two types of perspectives that need to be developed:

- How are martial arts techniques and teaching methods evolving technically with respect to their origin?
- How are martial arts techniques and teaching methods adapting to changes in American society?

Start with the premise that martial arts are an intrinsic part of human development. The history of martial arts can be traced over many centuries across many cultures. Taking an evolutionary model as a guide, it is also reasonable to extrapolate:

- Martial arts development followed local needs determined by locally available technologies, cultural norms, and situations.
- There was parallel evolution across different styles of martial arts. That is, martial artists in different places and times independently

came up with similar understandings about conflict/warfare and the capabilities of the human body.

- Not all martial arts developed to the same degree of maturity or sophistication.
- Most martial arts styles became evolutionary dead ends and were ultimately lost. For example, the culture that supported them was extinguished, technology changes rendered them obsolete, or the culture that once supported them had changed and no longer had the need for them or no longer had the resources to invest in them.

The martial arts historian Donn Draeger has written some in-depth analyses about the evolution from classical martial arts to modern martial arts in Japan. Draeger's focus was on the evolution from *Bujitsu* (i.e., warrior methods/techniques) to *Budo* (i.e., the warrior's way of life.) Draeger's work is essential reading for any martial arts teachers who want to understand the evolution of martial arts by looking at the specific historical example of Japan. Japan is an interesting example of the evolution of martial arts, because the self-imposed isolation of the country in the 18th and 19th centuries preserved its feudal characteristics until the modern era. As a result, more of its martial arts traditions were preserved intact until modern times.

Taking a broader view, it is possible to say that the focus of martial arts has adjusted over time to match the changes in our daily lives. The original focus was on **survival** - killing enemies and not being killed. In some places in the world that situation, unfortunately, may still be the daily state of affairs. However, in contemporary America, modern martial arts focus on **living** rather then **survival**. The idea of contemporary martial arts practice is to harness the intensity and spirit of the older life-and-death training, in a controlled way, in order to create personal growth and a warrior spirit.

Without going into the specifics of any particular style or culture, it is possible to identify some trends in martial arts evolution. The term "trends" is used because there are always some evolutionary changes that appear at first to be going backwards or that don't easily fit into the classification system.

Consider that from the very beginning martial arts have provided utility value across several categories of benefits. These benefit categories include: self-defense, force-projection (the ability for a person to develop a significant "edge" in a physical conflict), physical fitness, self-discipline, peace of mind, mental toughness, mental agility, etc. Over time, the evolution of martial arts has been influenced by which categories of benefits have had the greater utilitarian value to the contemporary society.

It is generally the case that all martial arts originated out of the need to be successful in armed or unarmed struggles, in early times, largely before the adoption of modern weaponry. The idea was that the martial arts were the application of a systematic set of practiced skills that made an individual more effective in combative situations. Over the course of time, technology and machinery proved themselves to be better at providing the competitive edge and overtook this original primary purpose of martial arts training.

The key to understanding this transformation is that while the original purpose for martial arts was warfare and other forms of human conflict, those were never the only purposes. Consider that in feudal Japan when martial arts were actually important on the battlefield, Sumo was considered a sport and archery was a recreational pastime for the nobility. Likewise in ancient Greece martial activities like wrestling and javelin throwing were part of the ancient Olympics. In medieval Europe, people were entertained by tournaments where knights competed in various forms of martial arts. So even in times when martial arts techniques had great battlefield relevance, there were still other dimensions to martial arts training.

The converse is also true. Even in modern times where the battlefield utility of martial arts is considered insignificant, there are still situations where the tactical application of martial arts has day-to-day relevance. Examples of this involve police arrest techniques, corrections officer restraint techniques, and self-defense training in general.

Of course, there is still some need for unarmed self-defense, but the social context is different. Where in the past, the life-and-death aspects of martial arts were useful for the preservation of a society as part of the normal course of events, that situation no longer exists. Now the life-and-death aspect of martial arts is generally related to personal protection associated with the aberrations of criminal behavior.

The following chart depicts the shift in emphasis as martial arts evolved from earlier forms to the modern context.

	Original Tendency	Contemporary Tendency
Intrinsic Benefits	•Mortal conflict as an obligation to protect the social order	•Recreation / Sports •Passive Entertainment •Health / Fitness •Psychological / Sociological
Extrinsic Benefits	•Recreation / Sports •Passive Entertainment •Health / Fitness •Psychological / Sociological	•Mortal conflict for self-defense situations

Table 3: Evolution of the Martial Art Value Proposition

The mix of these different value propositions not only clarifies the historical evolution of martial arts, they also provide a perspective for understanding the relationships between different kinds of martial arts. The following diagram depicts a hypothetical situation where the relative benefits of some imaginary martial art style were all in equal proportion according to a set of hypothetical scales.

In this model, all martial arts are assumed, for the sake of argument, to have five dimensions to them. Each dimension represents a different part of the martial arts value proposition. Taking this approach, it is possible to look at different modern martial arts as having evolved differently to emphasize different aspects of the value proposition.

The next set of scenarios will not look at specific examples of actual martial arts styles, but rather look at how martial arts have evolved along different lines to address these different value niches in contemporary society.

Given this working assumption it is possible to examine what happens when different martial arts styles emphasize different dimensions.

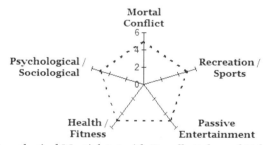

Figure 3: A Hypothetical Martial Art with Equally Balanced Value Proposition

The first value proposition for a martial art is its usefulness in mortal conflict. Emphasis on this characteristic is considered to be the norm for martial arts in the times before modern weaponry. One important point for martial arts teachers to remember is that even in early times, all of the other aspects of the value proposition were still present; the primary change over time is in the relative emphasis across the different aspects of the value proposition. Consider the following diagram which depicts a hypothetical martial arts style that has a primary focus on mortal conflict.

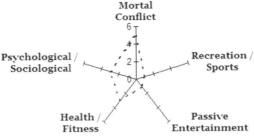

Figure 4: Hypothetical High Mortal Conflict Martial Arts Style

Another important point for martial arts teachers is that this while martial arts styles with this or a similar balance in their value propositions were common historically, they have not disappeared entirely. Certainly most of today's martial arts tend to be balanced differently. However, there are still niche martial arts styles that are primarily tactical. These might include: military commando training, police arrest training, correction officer restraint technique training, general self-defense training, specialized rape prevention training, etc. There are also some niches where, for cultural preservation or other aesthetic reasons, a small number of classical battlefield martial arts are still practiced in something close to their original form.

One of the most popular value proposition balances for martial arts over time has been Recreation/Sports. Boxing, wrestling, archery and fencing have been popular crossover activities between martial arts and sports for many years. In modern times these have been joined by the sporting forms of Judo and Taekwondo. Usually, the popularity of these activities is much higher among its practitioners than the general public, so they emphasize the *Recreation/Sports* dimension, rather than the *Passive Entertainment* dimension. The lesson here for martial arts teachers is that potential students are likely to be influenced by experiences that they have had in sport-oriented martial arts. It is well worthwhile for a martial arts teacher to take the time to understand them.

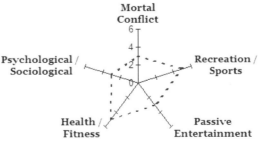

Figure 5: Hypothetical High Recreation/Sports Martial Arts Style

One thing that martial arts teachers might observe is that as students or potential students advance in age, their personal value proposition for martial arts practice changes. They are likely to place a higher weight on the *Health/Fitness* aspect of martial art training. Health and fitness can refer to strength, speed, coordination, balance, stamina, flexibility, and resistance to illness and the effects of aging. In earlier times there was a general recognition that martial arts training was good physical conditioning. In some cases like the Taoist philosophy in early China martial arts training was associated with broader aspects of health, even going to the point being semi-metaphysical. In contemporary America there are some martial arts derivatives that focus exclusively on the *Health/Fitness* aspects of martial arts. Take the example of martial arts aerobics. This is not something to be dismissed by martial arts teachers. They may be surprised to find that the martial art aerobic practitioners might have better stamina and cardio fitness than their own traditional martial arts students. It is also possible to find people practicing traditional martial arts primarily for reasons of *Health/Fitness*. An example of this is Tai Chi instruction at senior centers. This type of program would be primarily focus on a non-impact practice intended to benefit the participant in the areas of *Health/Fitness*. Martial arts teachers need to be aware of the motivations of their students and be conscious of when they are looking to reinforce or stretch those motivations.

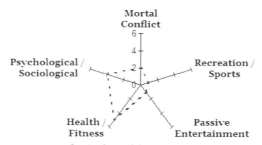

Figure 6: Hypothetical Health/Fitness Martial Arts Style

The mental aspects of martial arts have been recognized since early times. Some of these mental aspects are specific to the individual martial arts practitioner and are in the realm of psychology and even spirituality. Others deal with the martial arts in relation to society and are sociological forces.

The psychological aspects of the martial arts can be seen in demonstrations of mind-over-matter. Brick breaking, sword catching, and other martial arts demonstration techniques typify the effect of using the focused mind to control the body.

Another psychological aspect of the martial arts training is the meditative aspect. Rather then use the mind to control the body, the idea is to quiet the mind to make the body more relaxed and responsive. In general, the psychological aspects of martial arts practice have not changed much since earlier times.

The sociological aspects of martial arts go back to earlier times when martial arts were practiced within the context of a warrior society. In those times, society defined the social behavior of the martial artist. Training in martial arts was part of the rights of passage to enter into the warrior society. In modern times, that social support structure for martial art training does not exist in America. Martial arts teachers in contemporary America cannot take advantage of a supportive social system as was the case in the old warrior societies.

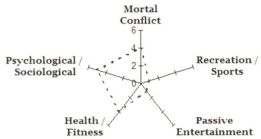

Figure 7: Hypothetical Psychological/Sociological Oriented Martial Arts Style

There appears to be an almost universal tendency for people to want to watch other people do something challenging or dangerous. Martial arts certainly appeal to that desire. The ancient Roman gladiatorial contests in the coliseum are a famous early example of this kind of voyeurism. Likewise, in contemporary America there are some noticeable examples of martial arts whose main contribution to their value proposition is passive entertainment. Martial arts teachers should not dismiss this too lightly. In contemporary American society, there is a lot of money in passive entertainment. The dedication by a society to that large of an amount of capital and energy deserves to be understood and respected.

Certainly professional wrestling and mixed martial arts are examples of martial arts with a leaning toward high passive entertainment. Naturally, mixed martial arts can also be seen as being a sport. The difference here between *Passive Entertainment* and *Recreation / Sports* is which side of the ring a person is on.

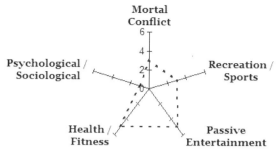

Figure 8: Hypothetical High Passive Entertainment Martial Arts Style

It should also be remembered that martial arts have always been an inspiration for the "fine arts". For example, in early times ritualized forms of dance have incorporated martial arts forms in their ceremonial and religious performances. Martial arts have also been part of the epic story telling that was so much a part of early human civilization. Throughout history, martial arts have been an inspiration for art and literature.

One aspect of the passive entertainment dimension which is unique to contemporary times is the prevalence of the video game. This is another follow-the-money lesson to be understood and acknowledged by martial arts instructors. Consider a generation of potential students full of hundreds or thousands of hours of simulated fighting experience, yet have never experienced meaningful physical training.

The martial arts did not arrive in the U.S. all at once. From whatever may have once existed of indigenous North American martial arts, very little, if any, has survived and authentically been passed down. The martial arts that are present in the U.S. have primarily come from abroad, in several waves. An early introduction of martial arts in the U.S. was Jujitsu demonstrations sponsored by Teddy Roosevelt at the White House.

A generation later, the U.S. was engaged in WWII. Large numbers of men were introduced to basic military Fairbairn/Sykes hand-to-hand combat training. More significantly, the occupation of the Japanese islands by allied military forces in the late 1940s through early 1960s presented unprecedented opportunities for Americans to study and bring back martial arts skills. This process was repeated a decade later during the Korean War and subsequent stationing of American military in Korea. In the 1970s Hollywood began to seriously embrace martial arts. Martial arts, which had earlier been a novelty or cult genera for the American cinema began to have main stream status, particularly those dealing with Chinese Kung Fu.

There are multiple good timelines available that trace the development of martial arts in general and in the U.S. in particular. Their differences are more a matter of emphasis and perspective, rather than fact. The objective here is not to retell the history of martial arts in the U.S., rather it is simply to establish the underlying principle that it has been an evolutionary process. The key take away points are:

- Martial arts were introduced into the U.S. incrementally.
- The world view of Americans was somewhat different during each wave of martial art introduction.
- U.S. exposure to the martial arts happened at two levels: the practitioner level and the common culture level.

The lesson here for martial arts teachers is to appreciate the evolutionary process and understand where they stand in it. Martial arts have their traditions, but the place for the martial arts teacher is in the present and not the past. Martial arts teachers are training their students in the present to prepare them for the future. Irrespective of martial arts style, it is the martial arts teacher's approach that has the greatest impact on the martial arts students. Without the correct sense of the course and speed of martial art evolution, it is difficult for martial arts teachers to strike the correct balance in their own personal teaching style.

Roles & Relationships

The study of martial arts is filled with irony and often confronts its adherents with enigmas and paradoxes. Among the most basic martial arts puzzles are:

    1) The role of the teacher
    2) The relationship between the student and the teacher

At some level of abstraction, the study of martial arts is a solitary pursuit of self-discovery. In popular martial arts mythology, we have come to think of the lone warrior on a training pilgrimage, or perhaps we conjure a vision of someone sitting in deep meditation, often in a lonely remote location, striving for the breakthrough to advance their understanding and technique. This concept is true, particularly at the higher levels of martial arts training. There are some famous historical examples of this in oriental martial arts. According to legend, the 15th century Japanese sword master, Iizasa Ienao, received a spiritual apparition after completing a 1000 days and nights of intensive training. The knowledge imparted to him by the spirits became the core teaching for his Tenshin Shoden Katori Shinto-ryu style of martial arts. In the 20th century, the Karate master, Mas Oyama, was famous for long periods of solitary training, including 14 months on Mt. Minobu and 18 months on Mt. Kiyosumi.

In contemporary America, intensive solo martial arts training such as that is rare. Much contemporary martial arts training takes place in group settings. As such, there are inherently social relationships present among the students and between the martial arts teacher and the students.

Our common culture tells us that the student's advancement is tied to a strong mentoring relationship with the teacher. This is often a key plot twist of popular movies like the *Karate Kid*, *Kung-Fu Panda*, and the *Teenage Mutant Ninja Turtles*.

Certainly there is information that can be learned without a teacher. This capability is greatly increased in the age of Google, Wikipedia, and Smart Phones. Computer-based modes of learning have advanced far beyond the early days of "distance learning" and continue to change the education and training landscapes. In the modern world, information is something that is in our pockets (i.e., smart phones), not in our heads.

This is even true in the martial arts. For example, high quality video clips of great masters, from around the world, both living and dead are available for our study with just the click of an internet button. In the recent past such knowledge would have been inaccessible, even with years of travel and training. We also see that video based group training classes can do a good job for certain martial arts variants, like martial arts derived cardio workout classes.

Yet, we are far from eliminating teachers altogether in the martial arts. Remember, even top performing professional athletes have coaches. Here are just a few reasons why teachers are still needed in the martial arts:

- **The student needs the teacher's observations** - At the level of physical training, students cannot accurately perceive their own movements. When they try to watch their own movements, they inherently change their head position, point of focus, and center of gravity. Just as in science, the act of observation cannot avoid influencing the outcome of an experiment, so it is in the martial arts. This act of self-observation essentially destroys the execution of technique. We sometimes try to minimize this by the use of mirrors or delayed video feedback. However, while helpful these tools also have their own limitations. The trained eye of the teacher is what is often needed.

- **The student needs the teacher's judgment and feedback** - Student are often not capable of recognizing the source of their mistakes on their own. The very lethal nature of martial arts techniques and the possible situations in which they might be used makes the trial-and-error and self-discovery methods of error correction inappropriate in many cases. The student should not be expected to know the appropriate type of correction needed to fix their mistakes. There may be several ways to correct a problem and one would not expect that the student always has the knowledge to be aware of them all or the discrimination to select the optimum one.

- **The student needs the teacher's wisdom** – Martial arts techniques do not exist in isolation. Typically a given martial art technique will have both martial and a pedagogic context. Martially speaking, there is always an overt martial context for a technique. That overt context addresses the basic question: "What do we do this for?" The student will usually intuitively understand the overt context, i.e., that when the attacker does X the defender does Y. However, for every technique there are usually multiple hidden contexts. For example, a given technique may be performed a certain way to position the defender from a possible second assault by a different attacker from the opposite direction. These hidden contexts address the more subtle question of: "Why do we do it this way?" The teacher needs to decide when to broaden the student's awareness with this additional information and when to let them focus solely on the more basic overt context. From a pedagogic context, it may be the case that the technique is being selected or taught in a certain way to emphasize the development of a certain skill or capability. For instance a technique may be performed a certain way because it develops a particular muscular strength and coordination that will be needed for the student to learn some other technique in the future. The student cannot be expected to have the foresight to understand these things for themselves and engage in self-directive training. This kind of direction requires a teacher.

- ***The student needs the teacher's inspiration*** - Traditionally, martial arts teachers are role models for relating martial arts to our daily lives. The martial arts students may not know what they do not yet know. However, they can see their martial arts teachers display behaviors that they can model in the hope of future understanding. In spite of all the technical advances in distance learning and self-guided learning, the fact remains that the human brain is pre-adapted to learn by imitation of socially significant role models.

- ***The student needs the teacher's discipline*** –The martial arts teacher is in a unique position to influence the relative balance between a martial arts students' physical and psychological progress. By way of a woodworking analogy: if discipline is the glue that binds a martial arts student's physical and psychological development, then the martial arts teacher's discipline is the clamp that holds things in place until the glue sets.

In traditional oriental martial arts, the teacher-student relationship is based on a Confucian point of view. In this Confucian perspective, the role of a teacher is viewed in the context of a special social interaction.

Confucian scholars made a science of defining the different kinds of relationships and it is worthwhile to consider what they came up with. They identified five major hierarchical relationships that they believed characterized a well-ordered society:

- ruler - subject
- parent - child
- older sibling - younger sibling
- husband - wife
- older friend - younger friend

These roles were fairly exclusive such that even in a situation where multiple roles might apply, only one role would dominate in that particular circumstance. The good order of society and the harmony of nature depended on understanding the correct role with respect to oneself and other people.

In contemporary American culture, the perception of the teacher-student relationship is often colored by the context of a supplier-consumer relationship. Perhaps this is due to American infatuation with an idealized concept of free market capitalism, individualism, and social Darwinism. There is an implication in American thinking that knowledge is a commodity and that as such, it can be rightfully purchased from a knowledge vendor.

There may be some value to this mindset; particularly for certain types of training. For example, when the goal is the simple transfer of information or acquiring simple skills, then the supplier-consumer model can work very well. However, information is not knowledge. *Knowledge* is *information* plus *understanding*. Furthermore, if the goal is the transformation of the student, then the supplier-consumer relationship is no longer the most useful way to frame the relationship. In this situation, the teacher needs to have a relationship role of *leader* or at least *trusted advisor*.

This is the way it is with traditional martial arts. The transmission of martial arts knowledge is not so much about the transfer of information as it is about transformation and creating profound changes in the student. So in keeping with that understanding, even today the traditional martial arts teacher-student relationship still retains a strong resemblance to the old Confucian model.

Usually, we would think of the teacher-student relationship following the parent-child metaphor. This is generally true when the role of teacher is superimposed on that of the head of a particular school or dojo. The reason for this is that the dojo head or chief instructor has the longitudinal responsibility for the course of the student's development, extending over countless training sessions and progressing through many ranks. This is much like the guiding responsibility that a parent has to raise a child to adulthood.

Sometimes a teacher may be an associate or assistant teacher at a particular school or dojo. In this case the scope of the teachers' responsibility is less and the relationship model changes to more of an older sibling – younger sibling model. This also represents the role of visiting or guest instructor. It is also characteristic of the *sempai-kohai* relationship between all senior and junior students. These "helper" instructors do not have the same longitudinal responsibility of a student's overall progress. However, they have key roles related to inspiring, motivating, and teaching their juniors.

Another possibility is the case of a very senior master-teacher who is also the head of a martial arts style and has many institutional responsibilities. This can be something like a ruler-subject relationship between the teacher and some of the students. However, the main focus here is on the day-to-day relationships between the student and the chief instructor and the assistant instructors.

The key points for martial arts teachers to remember are:

- Contemporary martial arts students have access to an unprecedented wealth of diverse martial art information from the internet.
- While it is expected that the martial arts student will be doing some amount of self-guided development and discovery, the role of the martial arts teacher is still essential.
- The relationship between martial arts teachers and their students can take multiple forms and the teacher and student should be aware of and work effectively within the boundaries of those relationships.

Traditional Pedagogy

Martial arts pedagogy is a mixture of traditional methods and modern thinking. Some traditional teaching methods are cultural baggage. Other than being briefly explored for historical understanding, they are best left behind. Likewise, our modern teaching methods are constantly evolving and sometimes seem to be as much art as science. Careful attention must be paid to selecting those modern methods which most closely complement traditional martial arts training and development.

There are a couple of key concepts in traditional martial arts pedagogy that are worth noting and they are characterized by these quotes:

> *The teacher is the needle; the student is the thread.*
> - Miyamoto Musashi
>
> *The student must steal the technique from the teacher.*
> - Traditional

In both of these quotes:

- The responsibility for insight rests squarely on the student
- The martial arts teacher's role is based on modeling and leading by example

In this light, the martial arts teacher never spoon-feeds the student. Neither can the martial arts teacher truly connect-the-dots for the student. What the martial arts teacher does is create a continuous series of scenarios where the student is placed in various situations where their self-realization, through execution of the technique, becomes more probable.

In traditional martial arts training, typically there is almost no conversation during a class, very little verbal encouragement, and certainly no unrelated small talk. Students learn to pick up their martial arts teacher's coaching through non-verbal signal. This method of teaching reinforces the training for picking up the non-verbal signals from one's opponent.

In some traditional martial arts instruction, the martial arts teacher demonstrates a technique with little or no verbal explanation. The instruction is based on the martial arts teacher's demonstrations of stylized executions of technique. This method of instruction takes the form of acting out a story, similar to a silent movie or pantomime. The martial arts teacher may demonstrate a technique and also include variations, so that the student may understand its range of application. However, the martial arts teacher may just as likely demonstrate a technique and then create a contrast, by demonstrating other options so as to call attention to their differences. It is the student's responsibility to train their perception, to watch the martial arts teacher's silent instruction, understand its meaning, and then practice it.

Training this formal is something that each student should be prepared for. However, it is not a method that is appropriate for modern martial arts teachers to use 100% of the time during every class.

One of the criticisms of the traditional approach is that it primarily teaches to the top 10% of the class. These are the students with the highest kinesthetic intelligence. The rest of the class is likely to be somewhat lost. Another consideration is that in contemporary American culture, verbal encouragement, directive guidance, and technical clarification during practice are essential parts of maximizing the learning experience. This is not just a cultural pattern; rather it is also based on progressive understanding of the psychology of learning. The older methods are simply suboptimal.

However, there are still some take away points from the traditional approach. Both the martial arts teachers and students must be aware that the primary emphasis of training is on observation and replication, not explanations and certainly not distractions. Martial arts training is an experiential phenomenon, not an intellectual pastime. Much of the technical discussion can be saved for after class or inserted by the teacher to give the students a break during class. Students and martial arts teachers must not interrupt the physical practice of the technique and the mental concentration that goes with it.

In those situations where the martial arts teacher decides to intervene with directive guidance or technical clarification, it should be a positive correction if possible. Remember the coaching about not hitting one's finger with a hammer. If a person places their focus on the nail head and does not think about their fingers, then they are unlikely to hit their fingers. When a person thinks about not hitting their fingers, they are actually much more likely to hit their fingers because they have fingers, rather then nails on their mind and the hammer will deviate to their alternate place of concentration. The martial arts teachers' directive guidance or technical clarification should move the student's mind to the nail head, not to their fingers.

The martial arts teacher does not need to correct every mistake of the student. If a student is making an inconsistent series of mistakes, the martial arts teacher will often want to wait until the student collects their mind and starts to perform consistently.

If the martial arts teacher does intervene, it will be to interrupt the student's chaos and simply break down the technique and demonstrate the components of the correct form. The experienced martial arts teacher will avoid applying technical corrections to a student who is making different mistakes on each technique execution. That approach would only overwhelm the student with a series of new things to think about. By allowing the student to develop a pattern, the experienced martial arts teacher creates a situation where one technical correction will alter a pattern of movement, rather than arbitrarily adjusting each isolated phenomenon. This kind of approach is not unique to the martial arts and is common for teaching different sports techniques like golf and baseball batting swings.

The experienced martial arts teacher will understand the kind of mistakes that a student is making. Some mistakes are appropriate for a student's grade level. Some mistakes are more subtle and sophisticated and actually show the teacher that the student is performing above grade level. Some mistakes are foolish and indicate that the student is temporarily confounded and performing below grade level. The martial arts teacher should give the highest priority to fixing those mistakes which show that students are currently performing below their level. Likewise students whose mistakes indicate that they are performing above grade level should be reminded not to be discouraged that they are falling short of perfection.

The best martial arts teachers have the ability to be restrained and selective in their corrections. During the practice of a technique, the martial arts teacher will observe the student's practice and perhaps make only one correction, but it will be a correction which makes a very significant improvement in the student's performance. Ideally the student will then have only one new thing to learn and remember from that particular practice session and will carry that correction forward for a long time.

Modes of Explanation

Many people who have practiced martial arts have heard the traditional stories of teachers using oblique or enigmatic methods to create a breakthrough in a student's understanding. Often these stories are from the Zen Buddhist tradition of Chinese and Japanese martial arts. Typically they involve the student being required to pursue some apparently extraneous activity and the teacher punctuating the situation with a seemingly outrageous interjection.

There is no need to reject the well-documented phenomenological effect of such esoteric teaching devices. However, they are very specialized and are only effective on rare occasions. They really only apply when the teacher is very advanced in a philosophic discipline such as Zen, the student is likewise inclined to be receptive to a counterintuitive instruction, and the physical opportunity for a object lesson has presented itself.

For the vast majority of teaching situations, American martial arts teachers are typical Americans with typical students (e.g., not Zen Buddhist adherents) and the teachers must rely on standard teaching approaches. Of course, having mostly "typical" American students does not solve the teaching problem. This is because the art of teaching is still not yet entirely a science.

Consider that in spite of the graduation, over the years, of thousands of Ph.D.s and Ed.D.s, the U.S. still does not have a consensus on how to produce either an educated workforce or electorate. When it comes to physical education, America seems to know even less, as its population is becoming more sedentary over time. So it might seem that martial arts education is the flea on the tail of the dog when it comes to the overall science of education.

Fortunately, martial arts come with their own tradition of training methods. Also, in those areas where educational science does become more advanced, martial arts teachers can capitalize on those advances. Still, the teacher will need to bridge gaps because, depending on the style, the traditional martial pedagogy was developed in other cultures and another eras.

One of the most basic educational challenges that a martial arts teacher has is to explain a technique to a student. In the old days, this was not necessarily a problem. In traditional martial arts pedagogy there might be little or no explanation. What the teacher would do instead is to model the move and the student would imitate. With endless repetition over time the student might, over time, come to understand:

1. Extrinsic physical characteristics of the move
2. Contextual application of the move

3. Intrinsic relationship between the move and other aspects of the martial art style from which it comes

It is difficult to determine how effective traditional martial arts pedagogy was. The focus of many of the available historical records is slanted toward the high-achievers to whom leadership of the art was handed down.

In contemporary America, worrying about the continuation of the style is not typically the martial arts teacher's problem. Most martial arts teachers are not the head of a style or trying to find the perfect successor. Martial arts styles in the U.S. are typically well established, encompass many school franchises, and leadership succession is not the concern of individual teachers. Also martial arts styles in the U.S. have been moving away from charismatic leadership by a founder followed by a string of successors. The contemporary governance trend in U.S. martial arts styles is more egalitarian and leadership of the martial arts style is more likely handled via a board of directors style of management.

Most martial arts instruction in the U.S. deals with more mundane aspects of teaching average students. This is sometimes referred to as "teaching to the middle", e.g., explaining a technique to an average student.

There are two important, and sometimes opposing, dynamics when trying to explain a technique to a student:
1. Reaching the student, at the most effective level, so that their immediate performance of the technique will be improved and their learning will be self-rewarding and self-reinforcing.
2. Acculturating the student to the way of thinking for that particular martial arts style so the context for understanding all other techniques is advanced.

To illustrate the dimensions involved in explaining a martial arts technique, consider five modes that the teacher can use to communicate with the student in order to explain a martial arts technique to a student. These dimensions are consistent across most, if not all, martial arts.

These modes are:

- Martial Awareness
- Physical Dynamics
- Kinesthetic Underpinnings
- Mental Integration
- Symbolic Imagery

Of course, this is only a model. So, it is possible to argue that there are 3 modes, or 7 modes, or some other number. The important point is that there are multiple modes that come into play when communicating an explanation.

When teaching a technique, the teacher needs to acquire the agility to shift between five modes of illustration. Generally, teachers will alternate between these modes and try to adjust their balance to match both the aesthetics of their particular styles and the existential needs of particular teaching situations for a specific class or with individual students.

The following graph depicts how all of these modes might look if they were given an equal relative weight on an imaginary scale of 0 through 6.

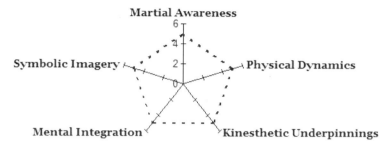

Figure 9: Explanation Modes

Individual martial artists may have differing ideas, based on their personal disposition and their styles, of what the proper balance between these dimensions should be. Also there are different philosophies for managing the time budget available for teaching (i.e., given limited class hours, what should be emphasized.) For example, the next two diagrams depict a potential difference in mode prioritization between a hypothetical "hard" style and "soft" style of martial arts.

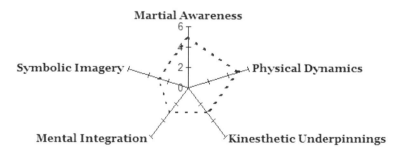

Figure 10: "Hard" Style

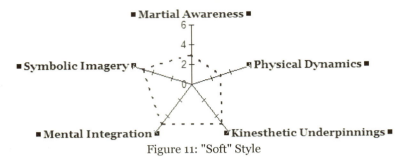

Figure 11: "Soft" Style

The important point is not what the specific weighting between these modes should be for a particular style. Rather, the point is that a martial arts instructor needs to be fluent in all of these modes with respect to his/her style. Perhaps the true genius of a good martial arts instructor is their ability to select the correct mode of explanation, at the right moment, for a particular student. When teachers are not adaptive and agile in their approach, instruction can become robotic and the effect on students will be proportionally deplorable.

Looking at these modes in more detail helps illustrate how they influence the martial arts teacher's explanation of technique.

Martial Awareness

All martial arts training is about perceiving and dealing with a threat. In tactical situations, this may mean overcoming an opponent by guile and force. It might also mean using strategy and tactics to avoid the conflict when it is in your best interest to do so. Sometimes the conflict is an artificial one that has been created for training or recreational sport purposes. In these situations, dealing with a threat involves creating victory within a set of safety rules. Superficially, this involves the ability to dynamically perceive and adjust to the self-defense possibilities presented in any tactical situation.

To truly understand this, a martial arts teacher must be familiar with the basics of Game Theory. Real martial art strategy simply can not be understood without a basic appreciation of Game Theory. Certainly, even martial classics like Niccolò Machiavelli's *Art of War* (1520 C.E.) and Sun Tzu's *Art of War* (circa 500 B.C.E.) can be much better understood by the application of modern Game Theory analysis. While much of the intricacies of Game Theory are beyond the scope of this book, one does not necessarily need to be a command officer at the U.S. Naval War College to grasp the principles.

Basically, Game Theory teaches us that there are some situations where there is a winner and a loser (*Win-Lose*) and there are other situations where there can be either multiple winners (*Win-Win*) or no winners (*Lose-Lose*). Our behavior in any of those situations is affected by the interaction of the adversaries in the game, based on their subjective outlook. In some cases, there are overlapping contexts which superimpose different Game Theory scenarios (*Win-Win* at one level and simultaneously *Win-Lose* at another level.) So as a martial arts teacher, one must be able to understand how the martial context applies to the immediate activity of the students.

These concepts should resonate with martial arts teachers who are familiar with Japanese fencing where similar constructs exist, but without the mathematical analysis associated with game theory.

Game Theory Classification	Japanese Fencing Concept	Meaning
Win-Win	Katsujinken	The life-giving sword
Win-Lose	Satsujinken	The killing sword
Lose-Lose	Ai uchi	Mutual kill

Table 4: Game Theory and Japanese Fencing

Sometimes, the martial arts context causes different game strategies to come in or out of play. The result is that the martial arts student is developing different martial arts awarenesses depending on the training situation. The following table depicts the different level of martial awareness depending on some common situations that are simulated in martial arts training in the light of game theory.

Martial Awareness Considerations		Game Theory Classification	
		Zero Sum (Win-Win)	Non-Zero Sum (Win-Lose)
Safety Constraints	Yes	*Practice Drills*	*Sport Contests*
	No	*Opportunity to Avoid Conflict*	*Life-or-Death Struggle*

Table 5: Martial Awareness

In the context of teaching, martial awareness means that the martial arts students are aware of the martial context of the particular technique that they are practicing. By explaining the martial context of the technique, martial arts teachers hope to make their students' execution of the technique more correct. Since the student will better understand the contextual use of the technique, the hope is that the instructor will not need to explain the details of complex physical movements. Instead, the appreciation of the martial objective of the technique will help the student internalize the correct movement with less explanation.

Martial arts teachers must watch that their students do not pursue the execution of a technique to the exclusion of its martial appropriateness. This would be the case when the student tries so hard to perform a particular strike or throw, that the student compromises the form, thereby exposing that student to potential counter attacks that should not be applicable to that technique. Note: this might include counter attacks that are not considered "appropriate" in that particular style/school. Certainly the student will want to win or get the technique right. However, the student might succeed in a technique because of a flaw in their training partner's movements. This situation might cause the student to misapply the technique and still get results. This chain of events creates a dysfunctional learning situation because it rewards the student for incorrect behavior and it requires instructor intervention.

This is particularly true for junior students and is part of the natural process of teaching and learning. However, it must never go unobserved by the martial arts instructor.

Likewise the teacher must stress the importance of understanding of the martial limitations (i.e., vulnerabilities) of each technique. Students should not be allowed to become overconfident of their martial knowledge. Their pride in their progress must be tempered by humility so that it does not become arrogance. A teacher who was teaching both Karate (a non-contact style) and Judo was interviewed by a magazine about the difference between the arts. The teacher responded that in Judo, "You always know what you know." The teacher's point that was in his style of Judo, practice in kata training was balanced by free practice where the relative mastery of a technique was tested in a contest with a clear winner and loser. However, in other martial arts, many of the techniques are not suitable for this type of practice. Even if there is some kind of competition, there are typically limits on what techniques can be practiced in this way. It can therefore be desirable for the teacher to specifically make a point to show the student that even when a technique is executed perfectly, there are still higher levels of the art where there are additional countermeasures that will overcome it. It is not necessary that the student immediately understands or begins to practice those more advanced countermeasures, only to understand that they exist and at some future point the student will be exposed to them.

There was a movie scene of an army drill instructor that had his platoon out digging fox holes. After the soldiers had worked diligently to dig the fox holes, the drill instructor had each soldier get in their hole. Then, to the soldiers' surprise, the drill instructor called up a tank and told the soldiers to "hunker down" while the tank drove over their foxholes. After the tank passed, the soldiers were elated that they were able to dig such good fortifications that they could endure even a tank. The drill instructor then called the soldiers out of their fox holes and called back the tank. At the drill instructor's command, the tank shifted its transmission and instead of passing over the now empty fox holes, the tank treads tore up the ground and destroyed the foxholes. So in this story, the drill instructor made two points about martial awareness. The first point proved that proper technique, in this case digging a good fox hole, made a good defense. The second point was that a good fox hole has limitations and is not always enough to protect your life.

Much of the time budget in martial art classes is spent on conditioning exercises or breaking techniques down into individual steps which are practiced and drilled in isolation. The martial arts teacher will want to remind the students that even these must be practiced with martial awareness. Of course, these elementary movements do not have a complete attack and defense theory behind them. However, martial awareness extends well beyond fighting tactics. Essential concepts of balance, extension, relaxation, focus, and awareness must always be maintained. By reminding martial arts students to exhibit these characteristics, even during exercises, the martial arts teacher is better preparing the students to take martial awareness into their everyday lives.

Often martial arts students think that at the advanced level, martial awareness means that:

- Even innocuous everyday objects and every body part is a potential weapon
- Any weapon (e.g., fist, foot, knife, club, etc.) used by an attacker becomes a weapon to be controlled and used against them

This is certainly true. However, it is the martial art teachers' mission to communicate that martial awareness is more than the systematic or scientific application of violence. Rather it is the more fundamental, and valuable, understanding of the application of resourcefulness and cause and effect in contested situations.

Physical Dynamics

If martial awareness is the most fundamental mode for explaining martial arts movements, physical dynamics is the most basic. Martial arts movements are all subject to the laws of physics. Above all else, the martial arts teacher must teach the physical pattern of the technique to the student. The physical dynamics mode uses a simplified view of the human body and its mechanics.

- Bodies move as solid units with respect to acceleration and momentum
- Joints bend according to simple mechanics (almost like marionettes or crash test dummies)

In the physical dynamics mode instruction focused on fundamental constructs and most of the instruction focuses on foot position, posture, and moving from point A to point B.

For example, think of a line drawing depicting a technique, such as a punch. It would communicate where to step, what arm to move where. The drawing might even be annotated with arrows that indicate direction or force vectors.

This mode involves a lot of physical modeling on the part of the martial arts teacher. Typically, the martial arts teacher will demonstrate a technique; perhaps the teacher will break the technique down into its fundamental movements and demonstrate those in isolation. The martial arts students will observe these gross movements and try to mental image. This is a little bit like the old time dance studios where the steps were taught by following sequenced footprints painted on the floor.

At the physical level this involves simple instructions such as moving the right or left foot and turning the body to the inside or outside. The martial arts teacher must communicate that we create structures with our bodies to deal with the natural forces of gravity, acceleration, centrifugal force, momentum, etc. People also create structures with their bodies to apply leverage, maintain balance, cover distance, create striking force, etc. In addition to creating structures with their bodies, people maintain physical relationships with their opponents by matching stance and distance or changing stance and distance. Once the martial arts student has been made aware of the martial scenario, the martial arts teacher must then communicate the gross movements and the body positioning.

Kinesthetic Underpinnings

This mode of explanation is the adaptation of gross movement and body structure to human anatomy and physiology. The martial arts teacher must communicate the concepts of relaxation and extension so that the techniques are natural and not robotic. The coordinated movement of muscle groups must be properly timed and sequenced. This begins to teach the martial arts student to understand the autonomic nervous system, muscle memory, and the body's tendency to dynamically realign its structure. It also introduces concepts about the opponent's own kinesthetic responses and how those reflexive responses can be utilized to control an opponent with far less force than the application of physics alone. This is where the physical application of *ki* or *chi* begins to apply.

Mental Awareness

Martial arts practice simulates events that are stressful. Even the act of practicing martial arts is itself stressful because it causes martial arts students to operate within interpersonal distances that they don't typically encounter in their every day lives. Typically these are close distances that leave martial arts students vulnerable to attack. In martial arts, the windows of opportunity for techniques are very small. The technique may have a spatial tolerance of less than an inch and a timing tolerance of a fraction of a second. A cluttered, distracted, or fearful mind will prevent successful execution of the technique. This is true at the gross physical level and it is especially true at the more refined level where there is an increased focus on the application of *ki* or *chi*. Martial arts teachers need to recognize when the student's state of mind is an impediment to their current grade level practice and make appropriate corrections.

Symbolic Imagery

Imagery has long been a part of martial art training. The names of various martial art techniques and styles are often based on metaphorical references that serve to trigger associations in the student's mind. A single martial art technique may require the coordinated movement of dozens or hundreds of muscles in a complex choreographed sequence. The teacher cannot explain all of this in words and the student typically cannot pick it all up by simply watching. However, by using various metaphors and imagery, the teacher can help the student build complex coordinated movements. The student's mind and body are already wired to perform certain set movement patterns and these are often associated with, and can be triggered through, mental imagery. The teacher must be adaptive at knowing when to insert imagery and realize that some images work better on some students than others.

The best way for the teacher to communicate these perspectives is to model them. The teacher should not overwhelm the student. It is better to emphasize one or sometimes two perspectives when a technique is taught and then wait until the next time a technique is taught to introduce a different way of looking at it.

It is easy to think that martial arts progress is incremental and that we progress from simple things to more complicated things, just as one advanced in elementary school from addition to multiplication to equations. This is not quite the learning model of martial arts. Typically during a martial arts class, junior and senior students all train together on the same techniques. For purposes of testing, techniques are separated by rank. This is not because they are simple or complex. Rather it is because the techniques are fundamental or composite. The idea behind testing students on techniques is that it provides an opportunity for the student to demonstrate mastery of one or more principles through the execution of the technique. Junior students do this with fundamental techniques; while more advanced students will use composite techniques to illustrate the application of combinations of principles. Martial artists will continue to refine a technique long after they have demonstrated it on an examination.

From a teaching perspective, there is always the challenge of the time budget. Given the number of class hours available for a student in a week, what will the teacher focus on? Naturally, most styles of martial arts prescribe some guidelines for the instructor. For example, white belt kata are different then black belt kata, in part because of their difficulty, but also because they are intended to teach different lessons that may require a different level of maturity for proper understanding. Sometimes this is referred to as the "hidden meaning" in a technique or kata.

However, the stylistic guidelines provided to the instructor are nominal. That is they are based on a typical class and the average student. It is the instructor's personal responsibly to personalize this to the level of each student in the class.

Sometimes a student's immediate learning problem might be within one dimension, but the correction can be expressed in another dimension.
For example, the traditional understanding of kata is that by "proper" repetition of a physical sequence of movement a breakthrough in mental awareness can eventually be achieved.

It is important for martial arts teachers to maintain awareness for whatever different modes of explanation they use in their martial art schools. Building on this awareness and refining it over time will allow the martial arts teachers to freely switch their instructions from one mode to another as dictated by the needs of their martial arts students.

From Context to Affectation

> ### *Affectation*
>
> Noun: *An attempt to assume or exhibit what is not natural or real; false display; artificial show. An unusual mannerism.*
>
> Synonyms: *unusual mannerism, eccentricity, mannerism*

Wiktionary

Martial arts are high context activities. Martial arts training is enmeshed in rules, traditions, rituals, conventions, mannerisms, theories, and stories that are used to communicate the underlying principles of martial arts.

Affectations occur when the martial artist does not appropriately discriminate between the essence of a principle and the contextual artifact that was used to transmit it. Sometimes an affectation can occur when a student attaches a value to an incidental contextual artifact that actually had nothing directly to do with the transmission of a principle, but rather was simple part of the overall contextual background. Since martial arts are so contextual and human learning makes such heavy use of associations, it is inherent that, from time to time, martial arts students, and even martial arts teachers will acquire affectations.

From the perspective of this discussion, there are three major types of affectation:

- *Cultural Affectation*
- *Stylistic Affectation*
- *Role Model Affectation*

The basis for *cultural affectations* has to do with the diverse ethnic and historical nature of various martial arts. Very often the origin of a martial art is from a culture that is not native to 21st century North America. Most martial arts practiced in the Unites States have been adopted from some other country. In addition, some of these martial arts are centuries old and have a cultural component which may no longer be found even within the contemporary culture of their country of origin.

Martial arts did not evolve in cultural vacuums and the external cultural context of a martial art is helpful both to the teacher and student. This cultural context includes aspects of the politics, religion, language, technology, and arts of the martial arts origin.

From the perspective of martial arts students, the cultural context of their martial art helps them see themselves as part of a larger community that transcends time and cultures. The martial arts students can appreciate that their training is conforming to time-honored methods that, when faithfully followed, yield consistent results. The martial arts students can also appreciate that their efforts make them part of a global fraternity of practitioners, both past and present.

From the martial arts teacher's perspective, the cultural context provides a way of explaining martial arts using time honored template-based lessons.

The cultural context also provides the students with a reference for relating martial arts training to daily life. Since daily life always occurs within cultural contexts, the stories, anecdotes, and conventions of a martial art's tradition provide a way of relating training activities to everyday life.

A famous example of leveraging cultural context can be seen in Miyamoto Musashi's <u>Book of Five Rings</u>. In this martial arts classic, Musashi draws many parallels between martial arts and other activities. In his description of the advancement of a martial artist from novice to master, Musashi compares it to the progress of a carpenter from apprentice to journeyman.

In most martial arts traditions, it is the teacher's job to educate the student to the relationships between martial arts training and everyday life. A well documented historical example of this can be found in the evolution of Japanese martial arts. Prior to the abolition of the Samurai class during the Meiji Restoration (1867 C.E.), the words used to name Japanese martial arts often ended in the suffix –*jutsu*, meaning *technique*. The abolition of the samurai class in Japan broke the institutionalized connection between martial arts and society at large. In the late 19th and early 20th century, this was a concern for certain individuals, including Jingoro Kano (Judo), Guchin Funicochi (Karate), and Morehei Ueshiba (Aikido). These people perceived that martial traditions were at risk of being lost. Their concern was not strictly in the preservation of arcane technical skills. They genuinely felt that the general society benefited from the collateral effects of martial arts training. As a result, they restructured the classical martial arts in such a way as to preserve this synergy. To emphasize this distinction, the names of the modern Japanese martial arts acquired the suffix –*do*, meaning *the way* and carrying the context both as "a path leading to a destination" and also "a way of life".

An over emphasis or over attachment to the cultural context of a martial art can actually impede learning. *Cultural affectation* occurs when martial artists misinterpret irrelevant aspects of a martial art's historical context for essential principles of that martial art. This false attachment causes a blockage in the martial arts student's development.

Stylistic affectation happens in much the same way. Martial arts styles and even individual martial arts schools within those styles all have certain ways of organizing and presenting material to their martial arts students. These conventions are followed by the martial arts teachers and over time become the teaching syllabus within those martial arts styles and schools. The value of these teaching traditions is that they are aids to help martial arts teachers communicate and help martial arts students to learn. Over time, new information and methods develop that have the potential to better deliver the martial arts' transformational message to the martial arts students. If the martial arts teacher is over attached to tradition, then there is more emphasis on historical preservation than on student transformation. That would be an example of *stylistic affectation*.

At the most fundamental and personal level is the relationship between the martial arts student and the martial arts teacher. Martial arts training typically makes heavy use of role modeling. As a result it is inevitable that the student would pick up certainly idiosyncrasies of the martial arts teacher. *Role model affectation* occurs when the martial arts student's fixations on these idiosyncrasies become a blockage to their proper development. Since the martial arts student is a reflection of the martial arts teacher, it is possible for the martial arts teachers to learn about themselves by observing and dealing with the *role model affectation* in their students.

Zen (Chan) Buddhist philosophy has long provided a world view context for certain martial arts. While not strictly a martial art example, this famous Zen story of Gutei's pointing is an in-depth study of context and affectation:

> *Gutei Isshi lived in China during the 9ᵗʰ century C.E. and became the 11ᵗʰ Zen patriarch. Tradition holds that Gutei spent his early days as a hermit monk, training alone in the mountains, focusing his meditations on the twenty-fifth chapter of the Lotus Sutra. One day, the junior monk was visited by a nun who lived nearby. The nun challenged young Gutei to a type of Zen Buddhist debate, known as "Dharma Combat". The nun's specific challenge was for Gutei to utter a single word of Zen. Young Gutei was not up to the task and could not compose his thoughts to give any response. Having spent so much time in meditation and study, Gutei became distraught at his own inability to say a single word of Zen in response to the nun.*
>
> *Gutei realized that his inability to answer the nun was due to his lack of understanding caused by insufficient preparation. Not long after that, a traveling Zen master passed through*

that area. Gutei approached him and implored the master to teach him. The master did not say a word and only held up his finger. At that very moment Gutei understood and became enlightened. Presumably because of these experiences, when Gutei himself became a master, he was noted to employ a unique teaching technique. Whenever Master Gutei was asked a question about Zen, he would respond first by raising a finger.

In time, Gutei became the abbot of the famous Shaolin temple and monastery. A boy, who was one of the attendants at that monastery, began to go about imitating Master Gutei in this way. When anyone asked the boy what his master had preached about that day, the boy would raise his finger. Master Gutei heard about the boy's mischief and eventually caught him in the act of mimicry. Master Gutei seized the boy, pulled out a knife, and immediately cut off the boy's finger. The boy, in shock and pain, started to dart off. Master Gutei called out and the master's penetrating voice stopped the boy in his tracks. When the boy turned his head to look back, Master Gutei raised up his own finger. The boy instinctively went to copy the gesture, but there was only a space where his finger would have been. Seeing that, the boy was instantly enlightened.

As with most Zen stories, this one is open to multiple interpretations. Certainly the mutilation of students, physically or otherwise, is not a desirable teaching practice in modern society and should be discouraged in martial arts for reasons of civil and criminal liability as well as both ethical and practical reasons. However this story is not without its symbolic value. The traveling master was able to discern Gutei's lack of natural talent for quick verbal responses. Rather than invest the effort to build up Gutei's ability for repartee, the master looked for a way to bypass Gutei's weak elocution. With great insight and perfect timing, the traveling master used his finger gesture to create a perfect teaching moment for the young Gutei. When Gutei became a master he took what had been a one time improvisation and successfully institutionalized it into his regular teaching. The finger was not yet an affectation because it was working for Gutei on a routine basis. However, the temple attendant was simply mimicking the physical gesture of Master Gutei. The boy had not understood the true context needed to make the gesture a powerful teaching tool and had reduced the behavior to the level of an affectation. In the end, Master Gutei also used great insight, perfect timing, and added severity to create another perfect teaching moment. Just as words had failed to work for the young Gutei, pointing had failed to work for the temple attendant. Just as Master Gutei, after his enlightenment, did not try to go back to relying on words, we are sure that after his own enlightenment, the temple attendant did not try to go back to pointing.

The purpose of telling this story is to remind the reader of the inevitability of martial arts teachers and their students periodically developing affectations. It is the responsibility of martial arts teachers to detect these affectations and help their martial arts students to move past them.

The Nature of Progress

All human accomplishments come with defects. Consider that Thomas Edison reputedly conducted thousands of experiments to create a functional incandescent light bulb. Even then, ongoing research and development has continued for many decades to attempt to perfect the concept. As a general rule, it is safe to assume that the advancement of progress is always imperfect. Sometimes this phenomenon is referred to as:

Two steps forward, one step back

Consider someone who wants to learn to throw a foot ball. The person can be taught how to hold the ball properly and how to move their arm properly. By itself, this does not mean that they can actually throw a football in any meaningful way. They may only be able to throw it from the couch to the coffee table (and miss the coffee table at that.) To be useful, the basic motions of the throw must be mastered against the demands of speed, distance, and accuracy. Now bend the rules of American football so that every bad throw results in the quarterback getting sacked and the analogy becomes more like the martial arts.

In the beginning of martial arts training, martial arts students learn by rote. They are copying moves that can eventually be repeated on demand. However, much like throwing the football from the couch, the moves have limited value outside of a training exercise in the dojo. In the beginning of martial arts training, the martial arts students never do the move correctly; they merely do it correctly for their level. With sufficient practice over time, the student acquires more balance, awareness, strength, speed, and accuracy. At that point the martial arts student can practice the same movement more correctly – appropriate for their now more advanced level. At this point, the martial arts teacher may choose to expand their repertoire by exposing them to more complex movements. This cycle continues throughout the course of martial arts training.

Unfortunately for the student, progress is seldom even. A student may show an improvement one time, but not understand how they produced it. As a result they may not yet be able to replicate it. Likewise a student's mental perception of their movement may mature somewhat faster than the refinement of their physical skill.

Both of those situations can be sources of frustration for martial arts students. Martial arts teachers need to help their students manage and master discouragement, so it is important that the student be properly taught what to expect in martial arts training. This can be expressed in many different ways because mmartial arts practice is truly multifaceted.

To prepare the martial arts student's ego to benefit from martial arts training, martial arts teachers need to cultivate the student's ability to learn by making them aware of the steps involved in making progress in martial arts practice:

- *Awareness that they are doing something wrong in their movement.*
- *Awareness that they have done something different than usual in their movement and that the difference is an improvement.*
- *Alertness to detect the difference when it eventually occurs again in their movement.*
- *Perception to understand the difference and incorporate it on demand in their movement.*
- *Maturity to realize that this process is both cyclic and integral to martial arts training.*

Capability, Affinity, & Commitment

Capability -
- *The power or ability to generate an outcome.*

Affinity -
- *A natural attraction or feeling of kinship to a person or thing.*

Commitment -
- *The act or an instance of committing, putting in charge, keeping, or trust.*
- *A promise or agreement to do something in the future.*
- *Being bound emotionally/intellectually to a course of action or to another person/other persons.*

Wiktionary

It is not a stretch to suggest that martial arts instructors have a belief that they are achieving some greater good as they develop their students.

At the present time, there is little in the way of systematic, scientific studies, to help guide martial arts teachers to understand how well that "good" is being achieved. Furthermore, that notion of "good" is likely manifested across a whole variety of different attributes.

As martial arts teachers evaluate their success, they must confront the issue of both quantity vs. quality.

Quantity is the easier dimension to measure: number of students enrolled, average length of training, number of promotions to various ranks.

Quality is more problematic to measure, or even evaluate. Martial arts teachers need to equip themselves with a systematic approach to evaluating the qualitative progress of their students. An additional complication is that not all students come to martial arts for the same reason and are looking to get the same things out of it. For example, a martial arts class may have a mix of some young adult students who are very interested in tournament competitions and some older adult students who are not at all interested in tournament advancement.

Realistically, most martial arts teachers are not running a Judo or Taekwondo camp for the national team, or some other elite program. Most martial arts teachers are dealing with students who have physical and mental limitations as well as significant constraints on their training time budget. So progress for a typical student might not be measured against some ultimate ideal, but rather how far that student has progressed from some point in the past.

There are many possible ways that martial arts teachers can think about this. To illustrate the point consider this model where the quality of a martial arts teacher's work is measured by three attributes of the students:

- *Capability*
- *Affinity*
- *Commitment*

Capability is the current potential of a student to train or perform martial arts techniques at a given level of competency. Capability takes into consideration both inherent aptitude and abilities enhanced through conditioning and training. Capability can be broken down even further and include multiple dimensions such as:

- Physical (strength, speed, agility, endurance)
- Neurological (reflexes, kinesthetic awareness)
- Psychological (spatial awareness, concentration, alertness)

Affinity refers to the fit between the personality of the student and the kind of activities that make up martial arts. Certainly martial arts cover a wide range of activities and people with very different personalities can find a place for themselves in the martial arts. However, the reverse is also true. Martial artists, particularly at the higher levels, tend to have a lot in common, even across different martial arts styles. Likewise, there are some personality types that are not well-suited to any martial art. For example, personalities demonstrating traits like laziness, apathy, and indecisiveness are not likely to be found among life-long martial artists.

Commitment refers to the time and effort that a student will dedicate to their martial arts study. This is not a simple calculation of the number of training hours that a student accumulates, but also a reflection of the quality of the effort expended during the time spent training.

Putting aside the traditional martial arts notions of belt rank, it is possible to imagine students progressing through a series of stages as they mature in their training across the three attributes of capability, affinity, and commitment.

Consider these categories as one way of describing the stages through which a martial arts student might progress:

- **Adherent** – Fully dedicated to all aspects of the way.

- **Booster** – A strong, reliable supporter and promoter.
- **Disciple** - An active follower. These students apply themselves intensively when they train.
- **Dilettante** – An amateur who claims an area of interest without real commitment or knowledge. These students are involved, but not yet fully committed to their training.
- **Transient** – A person with a fleeting interest. These students are neither involved nor committed at the present point in time.

Applying these classifications against the three quality attributes is illustrated in the table bellow.

Development Factors:	High	⇔ Development Scale ⇒					Low	
	Adherent	Booster	Disciple		Dilettante		Transient	
•**Capability**	High	Low	Low	High	Low	High	High	Low
•**Affinity**	High	High	Low	Low	High	High	Low	Low
•**Commitment**	High	High	High	High	Low	Low	Low	Low

Table 6: Development Maturity Scale for Martial Arts

A martial arts teacher could look at a distribution of students across these categories at some point in time and then repeat the exercise some months later. If a number of students were moving from right to left on the table, then that shows that those students are maturing in the martial arts and the martial arts teacher is can see some qualitative improvements.

Naturally, this is only an illustration. The important point behind it is that martial arts teachers must have clear ideas about qualitative progress in their students. For their teaching methods to continually improve, martial arts teachers must evaluate their qualitative results on an ongoing basis and make adjustments accordingly.

Section 2 – The Mind of the Teacher

Both martial arts teachers and their students are martial artists. Of course, this is less true of novice students or youth students who might just be testing the waters of martial arts. However, over time, and with perseverance, those students will also advance to the level where they are truly martial artists, irrespective of their becoming martial arts teachers.

Some martial arts teachers are lucky enough to have students who might excel at certain aspects of the martial arts and reach levels higher then their teachers. In fact, all martial arts teachers should aspire to produce a generation of students who excel them in some way - if not specifically as martial artists, then in some way as human beings.

Once there is an understanding that both the teacher and the student belong to the same community of martial artists, the question remains:

What is it that differentiates the martial arts teacher from the martial artist?

Ultimately, martial arts teachers have the additional responsibilities of transmission, i.e. passing on their knowledge in a way that shapes the lives of the students who receive it.

This section of the book will examine some of the perspectives and conundrums that occupy the mind of a martial arts teacher and signify the teacher's special role in the martial arts.

Why Teach?

It is very natural for some students who enter martial arts training to think that some day they might want to be a martial arts teacher. A common reason for this might be the mistaken belief that teaching is the highest level of attainment in the martial arts. It would not be a stretch to say that the martial arts teacher might appear glamorous to the more naïve student. Particularly for juvenile students, the martial arts teacher holds a power position and has a generalized persona of accomplishment and respect. As students mature, hopefully they develop a more balanced and better integrated attitude of respect that allows them to more appropriately contextualize the teacher-student role within the martial arts.

The object of martial arts teaching should not simply be a matter of attempting to be the "top dog" in some aspect of one's martial art. As some senior martial arts teachers will point out:

> *"Teaching is not a (rank) promotion.*
> *It is just added responsibility and more work."*

This is particularly true for martial arts teachers who are chief instructors and have full responsibilities for running a martial arts school (i.e., business operations, curriculum refinement, style conformance, direct teaching, and long-term student development.)

However, these additional responsibilities are not something that would necessarily be apparent to a junior student or a novice student viewing the martial arts teacher only from the perspective of attending class and training. After all, from a junior student's perspective, martial arts teachers appear to be spending more time doing what they love and receive compensation for it as well. In addition, there is a certain status associated with being a martial arts teacher.

Ironically, the time and effort spent teaching, often results in less time being available for the martial arts teacher's personal training.

Teaching is an outward focused activity where as martial arts training is inwardly focused. For some martial artists, the blend of inward and outward focus provided by teaching can be a good balance. Depending on the personal temperament and disposition of an individual martial artist, this may or may not be the case.

People sometimes have a tendency to project career outcomes based on simple extrapolation of a person's key interest or abilities. For example, if a child is intelligent and does well in school, some would say that the child should become a school teacher. If a child is reverent and does well in Sunday school, some would say that the child is cut out for the church ministry.

Likewise if a child is athletic and does well at sports, some would say that they should go into professional sports. There are some individuals who possess such passion and aptitude for an activity that they might want to center their professional life on it and make it into a career. However, this is not the norm. Certainly there are many very intelligent people who are not professional educators and many very pious people who are not in the ordained ministries and many gifted athletic people who are not in professional sports. The same is true with the martial arts.

Some motivations for teaching martial arts might be considered trivial or just inappropriate. For example, the desires to be popular or to be a tough guy both indicate an underdeveloped ego and would be dismissed as poor motivations to pursue martial arts teaching.

In general there are four commonly acceptable motivations for becoming a martial arts teacher.

- Circumstances
- Desire for Technical Understanding
- Alpha Drive
- Servant Spirit

Circumstances: Some martial artists have assumed the role of teacher simply because of circumstances. They begin their martial arts training and then reach some level of status as a senior student. At that point in their training they lose proximity with their martial arts teacher and they find that they have no alternative training venue. Perhaps their martial arts teacher relocated or stopped teaching, or perhaps the student relocated to an area with no suitable teacher. The end result is that teaching becomes the only mechanism for establishing and maintaining a martial arts training venue.

Desire for Technical Understanding: Teaching should compel martial arts teachers to constantly work to better understand the execution of their style's techniques. When demonstrating a technique, martial arts teachers not only need to be effective in their execution, they also need to be demonstrative. Their technique needs to be clear and clean so that the students can perceive the correct form, simply by observation. In addition to that, teachers need to have a clear cognitive understanding of the techniques so that they can verbally articulate the appropriate instructions, affirmations, and corrections. When diligently applied, such analysis will typically improve the martial arts teacher's own skills as a martial artist. Of course, being a teacher is not the only way, or even the best way of advancing technically. Simply upping the level of training will improve any martial artist's technical performance.

It should be noted that in some styles of martial arts, the teacher training program is the elite or "special forces" training for that style. Simply put, the most advanced and intensive training venues are reserved for the martial arts students in the teacher training program. These accelerated programs go by different names, including: *ukideshi* ("inside/house" student), *kensuchei* ("sword" bearer), or simply *teacher boot camp* programs. Some master teachers strive to devote their best efforts to the development of the next generation of teachers. Naturally, such a system will attract students who are looking to develop their own martial arts skills to the highest level, but not necessarily looking to apply themselves to the broader science of teaching. This is neither a flaw in the motivation of the master teacher or the student who seeks to experience the highest possible intensity level of training. It is simply a phenomenon to be aware of.

Alpha Drive: Human beings are social animals and one aspect of human nature is that people have a natural tendency to either want to lead or to not want to lead. The details and dynamics of these phenomena are subjects for social scientists. An inherent preference to lead is not a bad thing. In fact, from a martial arts perspective, a projection of leadership can sometimes defuse a conflict before it gets physical. Often times people who have a propensity to want to lead will pick out one or more aspects of their life and focus their desire for leadership in those arenas, rather than try to be a leader in all things, all of the time. For example, many martial arts students are presidents of companies, or deacons in their church, or hold other outside leadership positions and have no great personal desire to extend their leadership activities into martial arts teaching. In many modern corporate and political situations, leadership is a collaborative exercise in power and there are checks and balances which provide feedback so that leaders can alter their course.

However there are still many life situations - the martial arts school can be one of them - where leadership can be autocratic. Autocratic leadership is not bad in itself, if it fits the situation. For example, consider a person in a burning building, looking for an authority figure in a uniform to say "This way out!"

This also applies in more standard learning situations. Humans and other social animals have a natural instinct to identify leaders within their group and copy their behaviors. This is not simply a "monkey see, monkey do" form of imitation. It is a directed form of role modeling, where the focus is on emulating the most successful member of the group in an effort to achieve a similar level of success. This phenomenon explains why instructor-based learning has advantages over self-study methods for certain types of learning. This is particularly true when the teacher not only has the official functional role of "leader", but also is in fact perceived as the genuine "leader" in the social sense as well.

In a martial arts school, autocratic leadership simply means that there are fewer mechanisms for collaboration. For example, when teaching a class of children or raw beginners, the martial arts teacher has less opportunity for a collaborative leadership style and may benefit from a more Alpha style approach. In a school where there are many senior students who are functional adults, more collaboration is called for. First of all, it rewards the students by recognizing their growth and development. Secondly, the student body represents a collection of experiences and talent that the martial arts teacher can learn from. Finally, the martial arts teacher is trying to create thinkers and leaders. This means that at some point relative to their individual progress, the martial arts teacher wants to include those more senior students into some level of a collaborative leadership process. This allows the martial arts teacher to coach their senior students on leadership principles before turning them loose on their own students.

Lord Acton, a 19th century English politician and writer is attributed with the quote:

> *"Power tends to corrupt, and absolute power corrupts*
> *absolutely. Great men are almost always bad men."*

The martial arts teacher does not want their autocracy to become dysfunctional and slip into tyranny. In some Asian cultures where many contemporary martial arts originated, it may have been culturally acceptable for the authority of the teacher to be unquestionable and autocratic. Even when early martial arts teachers came from Asia to the U.S., some of them continued to follow that old style approach. However, for the contemporary American martial arts teacher, such a tendency is a serious flaw that leads to potentially bad consequences. In the *Karate Kid* movie series, a common sub plot revolves around "bad" martial arts teachers whose autocratic style was out of control. In contemporary America, highly autocratic approaches to martial arts teaching are perhaps best reserved for the specialized teaching of tactical martial arts classes for military and paramilitary populations of students where the sponsoring organizations have their own set of controls to provide oversight and prevent abuse.

Servant Spirit: This is the altruistic motivation for teaching. Certainly a martial arts school offers numerous opportunities for altruism apart from teaching. Just being a good student and paying dues on time is a tremendous contribution to the success of a school. There are also numerous volunteer opportunities to help out and contribute to the ongoing operation and improvement of a martial art school.

As it relates to being a martial arts teacher, this altruism may have different motivations. It could be a sense of gratitude and loyalty to past teachers. It could also be a sense of contributing something of value to the local community. It might even be a sense of cultural preservation based on pure love of a particular martial arts style.

An example of altruism is depicted by Eiji Yoshikawa in his novel <u>Musashi</u>, depicting the life of the famous fencing master. In one part of the novel Yoshikawa tells of Musashi entering the city of Edo to seek out an expert sword sharpener. Musashi approaches the shop of Zushino Kosuke and notices what he believes to be a calligraphy mistake/misspelling in the hand-painted sign above the shop. Instead of saying "Swords Sharpened" the calligraphy in the sign appears to say "Souls Sharpened". In Japan, the sword was often, is still referred to as the *Soul of the Samurai*. This gives the double entendre a special meaning in this story. When Musashi enters the shop and asks Zushino to polish his sword, Zushino examines the sword and then begins to analyze Musashi's life and character by the wear patterns on the sword. Musashi is puzzled by Zushino's reluctance to polish a sword for the simple purpose of making it cut better. Why would a samurai seek out a sword sharpener other than to make his sword a more deadly weapon? Zushino takes the time to educate Musashi:

> ...*First I'd like you to take another look at the sign on the front of my shop...you'll notice it doesn't say a word about polishing swords. My business is polishing the souls of the samurai who come in, not their weapons. People don't understand, but that is what I was taught when I studied sword polishing...*

In the context of this story, the sword not only represents the soul of the samurai, but is also representative of all the martial arts and the martial way (i.e., *budo*). This concept is reminiscent of the Proverb 27:17.

> *As iron sharpens iron, so one person sharpens another.*

A couple of points are worth mentioning. No one of these four motivations, by themselves, is a sufficient reason for being a martial arts teacher and certainly not sufficient for being a chief instructor. The first motivation of *Circumstance* is not an essential motivation, but there will always be some combination of the other three motivations. *The Desire for Technical Understanding* contributes a thirst for knowledge and a passion toward excellence. The *Alpha Drive* contributes a sense of ownership and accountability. The *Servant Spirit* contributes a sense of altruism and belief in a common good. During the teaching career of a martial arts instructor, the relative weight of these four motivations will change. The relative balance of these motivations will influence a martial arts teacher's style of teaching. As a result, martial arts teachers will want to reflect on their own motivations and think about how those motivations permeate their communications with their students.

The Periphery is the Center

There was an old saying among community organizers and political activists that goes:

Think Globally
Act Locally

The underlying concept is that while the root cause of a problem might be systemic, pervasive, and universal, our best tools for dealing with it are at hand, immediate, and self-directed.

Martial arts teachers quickly become familiar with this paradigm as they are confronted with the operational demands of teaching and running a martial arts school. The operational focus turns to what is at hand and what is happening at the moment.

The following diagram depicts how the typical focus of a martial arts teacher is centered on what they need to do at the moment due to the operational imperatives to act locally.

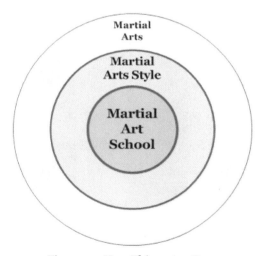

Figure 12: How Things Are Done

This depiction also makes intuitive sense because martial arts are transmitted through martial arts styles and the curriculums of those styles are delivered via martial arts schools. Therefore the school is the focal place *where the*

75

rubber meets the road (or perhaps more appropriately: *where the students meet the mat.*)

However, the teacher has a responsibility to see the big picture as well. This is the *think globally* part of the equation. It is also the responsibility of the teacher to stretch the students to see the bigger picture.

From the perspective of producing value and concentrating on what matters, the circles in the diagram become reversed. The more important lessons taught at the school are common to all martial arts because they are principles. These are things like balance, attitude, mental composure, and extension. The unique specifics of a martial arts style and even more so, a martial arts school, typically focus on small things around the nuance of executing a technique and the progressive practice of techniques within the curriculum.

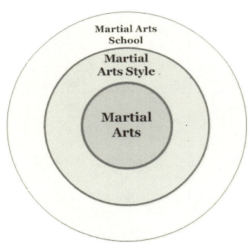

Figure 13: What Really Matters

This kind of inversion is not unique to the martial arts. A quick glance at the news will show that in many aspects of human endeavors this dichotomy gets out of balance. For example, many parts of the world are experiencing sectarian violence. How strange that people who share a core belief system should be in conflict over the details of their denominations, rather than embrace the core principles of their common underlying religion. There is a similar situation in contemporary American politics where a common sense of patriotism and political pragmatism (a.k.a. *Yankee Ingenuity*), has been stifled by ideological rigidity and political gridlock.

The martial arts teacher can help the student to develop an appropriate sense of awareness between the local and the global. Over time, this will help the student determine their own sense of balance between the two.

For example, when the martial arts teacher makes a point about the execution of a technique, the teacher could say:

"At our school, this is the way we do X, Y, and Z."

Or the teacher could just as easily say:

"In martial arts it is always important to consider X, Y, and Z."

Both statements may be correct but the first way is exclusive and the second way is inclusive. The first statement narrows the context of the martial arts teacher's message and the second statement expands that context. Just possibly, expanding the context and making it more inclusive will trigger additional connections in the student's mind and broaden the applicability and increase the value of the lesson.

Naturally, this presumes that martial arts teachers have such a sense of perspective themselves and the confidence to share it. This is not an easy thing because no martial arts teacher can be familiar with more than a small sampling of martial arts styles. The key point for the teacher is that learning every martial arts style is not an effective or appropriate way to understand the core of martial arts. A teacher can understand the core of all martial arts by mastering a single style if the teacher has the ability to abstract the principles and differentiate them from the specifics of technique, form, and teaching methodology. If martial arts teachers are not confident in this area then it is something that they need to make part of their own personal development plans.

This global-local paradigm has even broader applications for the martial arts teacher. When the martial arts teacher looks at the growth and development of the student, how should the martial arts teacher measure success? Certainly, a martial arts teacher can look at direct measures of a student's success. For example: tests passed, belts awarded, tournament trophies won, teachers certified, etc. However, this approach is exclusive and narrow in context. Also, the martial arts teacher has a certain capability to influence those numerical results by adjusting their standards and raising or lowering the bar.

There is an alternative model which looks at indirect measures of martial arts student success. The following diagram depicts a view that is more inclusive and expansive.

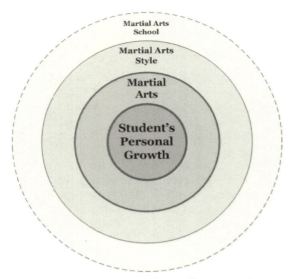

Figure 14: What Really, Really Matters?

Part of the "success" of martial arts training lies in what the student can do with the rest of their life as a result of their martial arts training. Consider the following examples of outside success by martial arts student:

- *A high school student who learns discipline and concentration improves and applies those skills to get better grades in school.*
- *A young adult who now spends more time training and less time in less desirable and possibly self-destructive behaviors.*
- *An older adult who gains the self-confidence to go back to school and earn a degree, take a leadership role in their church, or run for local political office.*
- *An adult who now understands that they can learn and accomplish new things and tries something new that they always wanted to do such as foreign travel or a business opportunity.*

In these examples, it may be that the martial arts student was not even a life-long student. It might have been that their martial arts training was quite limited and yet extremely significant and motivational.

Certainly it makes sense to say that if a martial arts school is delivering value, potential consumers/students will recognize this and the school will be economically sustainable and grow its enrollment. Likewise, it also is intuitive that the perception of the school's value on the part of students might lead some of them to become teachers and one would see a corresponding proliferation of affiliate schools descended from the original martial arts school.

This market theory of success has some truth in it, but is also limited in its applicability. The market theory presumes that the benefits valued by the consumer population are aligned by the benefits espoused by the teacher. The flaw here is that that the typical consumer's perceptions of value are not well informed when it comes to martial arts. For example, the potential consumer may not appreciate the amount of effort involved or the length of time needed to get a certain amount of value in return. So at best, there is only a partial alignment between what the population of potential consumers sees as value and what the martial arts teacher is offering as value.

A martial arts school which is a total commercial success is probably going to miss the mark in quality and depth as it seeks to develop a broader base of students who might be less dedicated to personal investment in change and growth. Likewise, a martial arts school can become so elitist that its wider social impact becomes completely marginalized and it becomes an evolutionary dead end.

The point here is that in the United States, the market test of value is real but not absolute. The martial arts teacher needs to understand where on that continuum they want their school to be.

Likewise that martial arts teacher needs to be aware that there are direct measures of success and indirect measures of success. The indirect measures of student success are harder to count, but it can be argued that ultimately they are more important. However, if martial arts teachers want to hold themselves accountable for fostering those indirect types of successes, then they need to be willing to go beyond a rote or mechanical style of teaching forms and look to engage their students on a deeper level.

Unintended Consequences

There is an old Zen story about a teacher. It is not about a martial arts teacher. Rather it is about an abbot (i.e., the head monk) of a monastery.

In earlier times monasteries honored a custom of hospitality whereby a traveler or pilgrim could always obtain a meal and a night's sleep in a safe place. Related to this was another custom whereby a wandering or mendicant monk could challenge the monastery's head monk to a religious debate (in the Zen tradition such a debate would be referred to as a dharma combat.) If the mendicant monk won the debate, he would be allowed to stay as a guest in that monastery as long as he desired. If the mendicant monk lost, he would still be able to receive the traditional one night's food and lodging under the general rule of hospitality. The mendicant would have nothing to lose and it might be that the custom was originally designed to keep the monastery abbots from getting lazy in their own spiritual development.

On one occasion, the abbot of a particular monastery had had an unusually long and difficult day sorting out the affairs of the monastery. Just as the abbot was looking for the relief of sleep, there was a knock on his door by a novice (i.e., junior monk) indicating that a mendicant monk had arrived at the monastery gate and was asking to engage in a debate. The abbot was so tired at that point that he did not care if the mendicant won the debate and became a resident guest. But the abbot did not even want to go through the motions of a half-hearted debate with this stranger and risk the potential embarrassment associated with losing. So the abbot got a clever idea. The junior monk who had brought the message was fairly new to the monastery. He was a young uneducated novice who had a very rough character and his face was disfigured by a missing eye. "Surely," thought the abbot, "if I send this ignorant novice to take my place in the dharma combat he will fail, but I can get some rest without needing to submit myself to this additional ordeal."

So the abbot told the junior monk to engage the visitor in the debate. Then as an afterthought the abbot added one instruction for the junior monk. Hoping to ensure for a quiet rest, the abbot instructed the junior monk to hold the debate in silence. The junior monk took his leave and the abbot settled in for the night.

Within a few minutes, there was another knock on the abbot's door. This time it was the mendicant monk. "I apologize for calling so late," said the mendicant monk. "I'll be leaving very early in the morning and I wanted to be sure to thank you and comment on the great debating skill of your young monk. You must be an extraordinary teacher. It has been a pleasure visiting."

The abbot was puzzled and asked, "What exactly happened in the debate?"

"Oh," said the mendicant monk. "We held the debate in silence, as I was told you had requested. I initiated the debate by holding up one finger representing the Buddha. Your associate responded back by holding up two fingers indicating the Buddha and his teachings. I naturally responded by holding up three fingers to indicate the Buddha, his teachings, and his followers. With that, your associate brilliantly won the debate by raising a closed hand to indicate that the Buddha, his teachings, and his followers are in fact all one." The mendicant monk then said his good bye and left the abbot's quarters.

A moment later the abbot heard footsteps running and up came the junior monk looking very agitated. "Where is that rude stranger? I am going to beat the daylights out of him!" Now the abbot was even more confused. "What exactly happened at the debate?" asked the abbot.

"Well," said the junior monk, "I instructed him that the debate should be held in silence as you requested. Then right off the bat this wise guy insulted me by raising up one finger to call me a one-eye. Given that he was a visitor I was willing to forgive his rudeness and I raised two fingers to let him know that I was happy for him to have two eyes. But he just would not stop! He then raised three fingers, indicating that between the two of us, we only had three eyes! So I shook my fist at him to let him know that once the debate was over, I was going to beat him up. Unfortunately, he suddenly disappeared. We never even got to debate! I've been searching the grounds looking for him to give him a thrashing."

As is the case with any good Zen story, there is never just one moral. One lesson of this story has to do with the relativity of perception. In martial arts, perception is the key. This leads martial arts practitioners to want to believe that perception can be absolute. However, ultimately the absolute decisions involving life and death are always based on relative perceptions.

However, the primary lesson here has to do with teachers and unintended consequences. In this story the abbot started to go astray by taking a lazy shortcut to avoid his duty. Technically, the abbot was within his rights to delegate the assignment. In most such delegation situations the intent would have been to give the designee a training opportunity to test their knowledge against a visitor. That was not the situation in this story.

Unintended consequences are anathema to the martial arts ethos. There is an old martial arts saying, attributed to the Japanese samurai warlord Toyotomi Hideyoshi:

"Fight only after creating the conditions for victory."

Fortunately in this story, everything works out in the end. The abbot learns his lesson, the visitor get an unintended enlightenment lesson, and the young monk does not get into a fight.

Apart from the issue of improper delegation by the abbot, the main point is that students will come up with the most interesting and sometimes outrageous interpretations of what it was they thought the teacher said or did. Even sincere, dedicated students will sometimes hold onto unusual and inappropriate concepts because they have mistakenly interpreted them from their martial arts teacher. In the older, traditional, teaching methods this might have been considered acceptable in the hope that eventually the student would: A) recognize the error, and B) be sharper the next time to avoid the embarrassment of being wrong.

This problem not only happens with individual students, it also happens with entire classes. Many times at a martial arts seminar, a guest teacher will demonstrate some technique in a certain way to make a specific point. After the demonstration by the guest teacher, the majority of the students are practicing the same way that they always have. Each student has interpreted what they saw from their own unique perspective of what they already know. At that point in the seminar, the practice becomes reminiscent of the proverb about the blind men trying to describe the elephant.

Finally there is the situation when the martial arts teacher is teaching without even being aware of it. A student may be observing the martial arts teacher answering the telephone, eating, sitting, walking, or doing some other mundane activity. It is expected that an advanced martial art practitioner is always martially aware. Certainly that is a difficult goal to achieve 100% of the time, but it is certainly a worthwhile personal goal for a martial arts practitioner to strive for. The martial arts practitioner strives to be martially aware regardless if they are in a martial situation or not. By extension, the same principle applies to a martial arts teacher. The martial arts teacher is in a teaching role whether they are leading a class or not. In fact, as long as there is even one student present, the martial arts teacher is teaching and needs to be aware of that.

In a modern view of teaching, martial arts teachers need to be clear and effective, both when physically modeling and verbally explaining the techniques of their martial arts styles. Martial arts teachers have the responsibility to narrow the range of possible variant interpretations that their students might come up with. Martial arts teachers then need to go further and test their student's understanding and then apply correction. The corrections should be made to the students to fix their understandings while the martial arts teachers themselves improve the effectiveness of their teaching methods. This all can be summarized in three steps for the teacher to minimize unintended consequences:

- Preparation of effective physical modeling and verbal explanation
- Validation of students' interpretation
- Refinement of the teaching method

The martial arts teacher would do well to paraphrase Hideyoshi's motto:

Teach, only after creating the conditions for effective learning.

Modeling vs. Showing Off

In practicing:
- *Do not show your strength without some good purpose lest you awaken resistance in the minds of those who are watching you.*
- *Do not argue about strength, but teach the right way. Words alone cannot explain. Sometimes by being the one to be thrown, you can teach more effectively.*
- *Do not halt your student's throw at mid-point or stop his Ki before he can complete a movement, or you will give him bad habits. Strive always by word and act to instill in him the correct Ki and the art of Aikido.*

From *12 Rules for Aikido Instructors*, Aikido in Daily Life by Koichi Tohei, 10th Dan

Human beings are social animals. Perhaps that is why people sometimes want to identify with the accomplishments of others. This is something that humans learn in their early development. In hunting/gathering societies such instinct enhances the ability of children to stay safe, bond with capable protectors, and acquire skills. Of course very young children are dependent and are not capable of producing accomplishments of utility to their community. They can only perform personal accomplishments that advance their development and edify their immediate family. As a child gets older and this instinct matures, the child seeks out role models and learns to bond with their social group. Sometimes a child may want to compete or achieve, but lacks the capability to do so. In these situations, young children identify with a group or an individual hero/champion and will say things like:

- *My dog is better then your dog.*
- *My brother can beat your brother.*

When people mature to adulthood and develop more sophisticated mechanisms for rationalizing the world, the childhood type of thinking becomes overlaid, but not replaced. When describing a child's mind, the term *hero worship* is used to express the affinity that they project onto other more capable individuals. As people develop and mature, they become more self-accomplished. At the same time, the scope of their affinity towards more capable people changes as it becomes more limited and rationalized. *Hero worship* becomes sublimated by more rational constructs like *role model* and *mentor*.

Of course the childhood construct of *hero worship* never truly goes away; it just stays in the background and occasionally moves into the foreground. Even normal adults sometimes get satisfaction from the accomplishments of others whom they have developed an affinity toward. A common example is the adulation which sports fans feel when their sports hero helps win a championship game. Of course, sometimes people get carried away and at some point, this natural tendency can become dysfunctional.

When people get satisfaction from the accomplishments of others this is referred to as a *vicarious accomplishment*. In the martial arts, this is a problem that teachers must be aware of. Martial arts teachers must be seen by their students as *role models* and *mentors*. They must not be the objects of *hero worship*. This is true even if the martial arts teacher is truely a world-class martial artist. The focus on martial arts training must be on the development of the student and enhancing the student's capabilities. When the student starts overly focusing on the martial arts teacher's accomplishments, the student can get the impression they will become accomplished martial artists by proxy.

In the Zen tradition, the following expression is used to describe this situation:

Putting a head on top of your own head.

The expression paints a ludicrous image of a person walking down the street while wearing a decapitated head as if it were a hat. When such a person addresses you, they would like to believe that they speak with the vicarious authority of whoever's head is stacked up on theirs. This is the situation where someone quotes an authority rather than speaking with the authority of understanding the underlying material.

Martial arts teachers should not want to see their students walking around with the teacher's head attached to the top of theirs, taking on the martial arts teacher's accomplishments as if they were their own.

Certainly it is expected that the martial arts teacher will usually have better technique than most of their students. It is also expected that the martial arts teachers always model the most correct form for their students. However, martial arts teachers should not be trying to impress their students. There is a big, but sometimes subtle, difference between *impressing* and *inspiring*. In this comparison, *impressing* is being used to describe the gratuitous demonstration of skill aimed at creating an attachment toward the martial arts teacher by the martial arts student.

Actually, in some marketing situations and public demonstrations, there may sometimes be a legitimate purpose for this kind of spectacle. However, in general, this kind of showing off is inappropriate. The martial arts teacher does not need to prove themselves to their students by demonstrating advanced technical proficiency which the students do not have the capability to evaluate. The need to do this on the part of the martial arts instructor suggests either a lack of personal confidence/esteem or a lack of presence /

leadership. *Inspiring*, in this comparison, refers to the demonstration of advanced capabilities, in order to provide the martial arts student with a model of higher level performance.

In this context, *impressing* may be seen as showing off. It may be motivated by the martial arts teacher's selfishness, and distracts the martial arts students from focusing on their own development. *Inspiring*, by contrast, can be seen as the modeling of excellence; it is a generous act by a confident martial arts teacher, and it is aimed at focusing the student's aspirations on a future level of accomplishment.

Preference & Bias

> *...You should not have a favorite weapon. To become overly attached with one type of weapon is as bad as not knowing it sufficiently well. You should not seek to imitate others, but use weapons which you can handle proficiently. It is bad for commanders and troopers to have likes and dislikes. Pragmatism is essential in these matters. These are things you must learn thoroughly...*
>
> A Book of Five Rings, Miyamoto Musashi

The martial arts are not empirical sciences. A martial arts teacher cannot point to an integrated body of facts, vetted by the scientific method, which will clearly detail the best way to teach. Certainly martial arts employ many facts that lend themselves to scientific analysis. For example, consider the following scenarios which have been successfully studied in various experimental and investigative ways:

- *What distance can an attacker with a bladed weapon close, before a defender with a holstered gun can draw, aim, and shoot?*
- *How many seconds of consciousness does a defender have when a particular choke / strangle hold is applied?*
- *Wounds to what parts of the body will produce an "instant" kill?*

The mechanical aspects of martial arts instruction can be full of scientifically testable facts. This aspect of the martial arts is subject to analysis by the physical sciences, but also subject to analysis from psychology, perception, physiology, sociology, and the full range of scientific disciplines.

However, a significant portion of martial arts practice and teaching does not rely as much on scientific facts as it does on scientific principles.

The greater focus of martial arts teachers and practitioners deals with the application of these principles to specific martial situations. Principles are more general than facts, but they are derived from facts. Some expressions of martial arts principles may include statements like:

- *Keep your body relaxed.*
- *Do not allow your eyes to fixate on your opponent's body.*
- *Control the center line.*

Certainly, much of the advice in this book concerning martial arts instruction is at the "principle" level of abstraction. Abstraction is the cognitive ability to associate physical things with conceptual things and associate conceptual things with other conceptual things. Abstract thinking allows people to mentally manipulate abstract concepts and infer what might happen to their physical counterparts.

The application of these principles to martial situations requires the use of various intellectual skills. Some of these abstract thinking tools include:

- *Deductive Reasoning*
- *Inductive Reasoning*
- *Generalization*
- *Extrapolation*

This requirement to apply these mental processes introduces a level of subjectivity into martial arts instruction. Everyone's application of these intellectual skills will be different and influenced by a variety of considerations.

Since subjective reasoning is unavoidable for martial arts teachers, they must be on guard for preference and bias. It is easy for the reasoning process to be corrupted by fears, desires, attachments, and prejudices. Sometimes martial arts teachers rely on subjective reasoning because it is appropriate to the situation. Here is an example of a subjective reason that is based on trust rather than empirical knowledge.

> *"In my style of martial arts, we traditionally perform this particular technique in this particular way. I have trust that the originators of my martial arts style knew what they were doing."*

In that example, the martial arts teacher did not yet reach the full understanding of the style. Yet, in order to teach, some decisions needed to be made about what and how to teach. That is fine; no martial arts teacher starts off as a master teacher with a full realization of their martial arts style. It is acceptable for martial arts teachers not always to know the reasons for everything to do with the martial arts.

What martial arts teachers need to be concerned about is the influence of negative subconscious motives that can create unrecognized bias in their teaching decisions. For example:

- *I want to avoid teaching techniques that I am uncomfortable with because I might not look impressive in front of my class.*

- *I want to avoid teaching techniques that don't gratify my students' egos and discourage their enrollment in the next semester's class.*
- *I want to avoid trying to teach techniques that I am not good at because I don't want to face up to my own continued need for growth and development.*

In the best case, martial arts teachers have empirical reasons for what they teach and how they teach it. However, martial arts are not an exact science. As a result, the martial arts teacher is often called on to make decisions based on balanced, but subjective, reasoning. In these situations, it is important that martial arts teachers balance their reasoning and examine themselves for any bias that might be motivated by dysfunctional or self-serving considerations.

The 100% Rule

Martial arts teachers commonly use the word *always*. Of course, this is an absolute and cannot be correct except in very limited circumstances. Typically, martial arts teachers use the word *always* as a hyperbole. It is a conscious exaggeration to make it easier for martial arts students to process and remember an instruction.

Take for example a martial arts truism:

> *Always be prepared for an additional attacker.*

Superficially, it seems to be a universal truth. Yet it can be readily seen that this is not always exactly the case. For example, the martial arts are full of submission and restraint techniques which would never be appropriate if there was a chance of a second attacker. Obviously, *always* does not literally mean *always*.

So when a martial arts teacher uses the term *always*, what is really meant?

Sometimes, when the martial arts teacher says *always*, the martial arts teacher really means:

> *Listen student, for your level of training and maturity, I want you to limit the focus of your attention to stay within these parameters.*

It is also possible that the martial arts teacher is not using the term *always* as an absolute, but rather as a relative term within a particular form or martial art style. For example, a Karate instructor may say something like this:

> *In the horse stance position of the Seiuchin kata, the feet are about shoulder width apart and the toes are always pointed out at a 45 degree angle.*

In that example, the context of always has been greatly narrowed. It is no longer being used as a truism. Rather, it is being applied as part of the inherent definition of a specific stance, within a specific kata, as it is interpreted by a particular style, within a particular martial art.

There is an old saying that the way of a warrior is like a mountain and there can be many paths to the top. Usually the saying is in reference to different martial arts. However, it can be taken down to the level of different styles within a martial art and eventually down to the specific teaching methods of individual instructors within the same martial arts style.

For martial arts students who are studying for only a limited time, it may not be important or even desirable that they are aware that there are other paths. Examples of this kind of situation would be tactical martial arts programs for military, police or correction recruits. The focus here is on using a limited time budget to teach a specific way of doing something.

The same is true for any novice student and for most pre-adult students. It is best to just focus on the basics of the style being taught and the interpretation of that dojo's chief instructor.

So for the novice students, juvenile students, or for the student in a fixed duration curriculum, the martial arts teacher can productively employ hyperbole and oversimplification as rhetorical devices to quickly deliver a basic message.

However, when students begin to transition into life-long practitioners, the martial arts teacher must be able to offer them something more. The martial arts teacher must be able to guide the life-long student from being merely a good stylist and lead them to become a well-rounded martial artist. For these more serious students, teachers can take the time to qualify their remarks and use context to change platitudes to principles that the martial arts students can build on.

In this situation the martial arts teacher might begin to say things like:

- *At our school, we **always** train with our foot in this position, **but** other teachers in our style teach it slightly differently.*

- *In practice we **always** enter this way on this technique, **but** that assumes that your opponent has martial awareness and responds appropriately. Outside of the dojo, your technique **may be different** because an untrained attacker might be oblivious to the danger that they face if they are in the wrong position.*

Naturally, the martial arts student may come back and say something like:

- *Well if other teachers teach it differently, is their way better?*

- *Well if it would work differently in the street, why do we practice this way?*

The martial arts teacher must know and be prepared to answer such questions. This is particularly true when the student has advanced to the point where they can appreciate the wisdom of the answers.

The martial arts teacher must understand the level and needs of the student that they are working with. Sometimes more expansive instructions are appropriate and sometimes less expansive, more directive instructions are appropriate. The choice of the most appropriate explanation should be based on the martial arts student's learning needs and not the personal proclivity of the martial arts teacher to be either verbally expansive or laconic. It is both acceptable and appropriate for martial arts teachers to use the word *always* in their instructions. The key point is that the teachers must understand whether they are talking about *always* as an absolute or using it as a hyperbole.

Communication Breakdown

There is a natural tendency to want to explain things clearly and completely, or as people sometimes say "in plain English". This is the kind of language which would be expected in a textbook or some type of manual. It is a particular mode of discourse known as *expository writing*. Expository writing is a particular type of writing where the purpose is to explain, inform, or describe. It often follows a pattern of explanation and analysis of information by the presentation of an idea, relevant evidence, and appropriate discussion.

Martial arts teachers have a responsibility to communicate accurately with students in a way that is both accurate and appropriate to the martial arts student's level of comprehension. Unfortunately, there are important aspects of martial arts that exceed the capacity of expository writing.

Natural languages, like American English, have significant limitations in trying to describe the manifest complexities of life in an absolutely accurate and unambiguous fashion.

When people have a need to be more precise in their communications, then they might switch from "plain English" to a synthetic language. The synthetic language might be an artificial language, like algebraic notation or a computer language. More commonly, people resort to specialized variants of English that are typically called jargon. Jargon is a specific extension to a language to address the needs of a functional domain. For example different professions and trades all have their own jargons. Lawyers, plumbers, policeman, carpenters, soldiers, and clergymen are just some examples of people who use specialized extensions to "plain English" to communicate more precisely and concisely about their subject. In learning jargon, people are exposed to multiple situations which imprint and reinforce the meaning of a term within a specific context. Those experiences load a lot of contextual meaning onto individual terms and jargon is helpful in describing details. While jargon can enhance the communication of people who share the prerequisite common experiences, it is not so effective at communicating with people outside of that group.

Certainly each style of martial arts has its own jargon. The problem for the martial arts teacher is that martial arts jargon can be very subtle and take years to master. Consider these two common terms in Japanese martial arts:

- *mushin* - "no mind" a mind not fixed or occupied by thought or emotion and thus open to everything
- *zanshin* - "remaining mind" a relaxed state of awareness at the completion of a move

93

These terms are used to explain mental attitudes that are subtly expressed through the body. As a result, martial arts teachers can more easily use jargon to communicate with experienced martial arts students, but cannot so readily apply it to more junior martial arts students or the non-martial arts community.

In addition to the inherent difficulty in describing things precisely, "plain English" also has limitations describing things that are ephemeral. For example, sensory experiences such as taste, touch; emotional experiences such as love, happiness, anger, admiration; spiritual experiences such as peacefulness, tranquility, centeredness; all of these experiences are difficult to describe objectively. When attempting to describe these experiences, people often resort to using language in a symbolic or abstract way. This might include modes of expression including: poetry, story telling, fables, anecdotes, and parables. It can also involve the use of rhetorical techniques like syllogisms, analogies, metaphors, etc. The notion behind these non-literal methods and techniques is that by relating the listener or reader through a scenario that they can understand, the listener or reader can then isolate the scenario's underlying principle and apply it back to the real area of interest.

Given the nature of the martial arts, it is important that martial arts teachers be skillful at moving between these different modes - sometimes explaining logically, sometimes using the shorthand explanations of their martial art style, and sometimes using the creative expression of story telling. It is to be expected that not all martial arts teachers are equally comfortable in each mode of communication. However, the selection of the most effective mode should depend on the particular need of the martial arts student, not the limitations of the martial arts teacher. As a result, martial arts teachers should always be developing their communication skills across all of the modes of explanation.

Teaching as Combat

It is important that the martial arts teacher maintains continuity between teaching martial arts and practicing martial arts. When the martial arts teacher is instructing the class, it is as if the martial arts teacher was taking on the entire class in combat. This is true regardless of the composition of the class - beginners or advanced, youth or adult.

This does not mean that the teacher-student relationship in a martial arts class is in anyway adversarial or even confrontational. Rather, it refers to the high levels of awareness and mental energy required of a martial arts teacher.

The martial arts teachers must always be aware of their entire class. They need to perceive every student's performance and process subtle, even subliminal, clues about each student's physical condition and state of mind. Naturally, this implies that the martial arts teacher's mind must be as clear and mirror-like when they are teaching as when they are practicing martial arts. Even when stopping to demonstrate or to correct a student, the martial arts teacher must not shut off their mind to the rest of the class. This is not the contemporary notion of multitasking or trying to do many thinks at once. Rather, it is the traditional martial arts concept of not letting one's mind get stuck or fixated on one matter to the exclusion of another. Certainly, if a martial artist is blocking an opponent's punch, then the martial artist cannot become fixated on the block such that awareness of the opponent's feet or other arm is lost. If that were the case, blocking the punch would only lead to getting hit in some other way. So just as a martial artist must keep their mind free to examine all of the continually changing options in a conflict, martial arts teachers must keep their minds clear to respond to the changing landscape of the students during a class.

There are two reasons why this is important to martial arts teachers.

The first reason is safety. Martial arts training is certainly not combat, but is does involve physical risk. So while the dojo may not be like a battlefield, it is certainly like a construction zone. The dojo has dangerous objects moving around at high speeds. For that reason 360 degree awareness is a prerequisite for everyone involved.

The second reason is that there should not be any difference between the mind set of the martial arts teacher as a teacher, as a martial artist, or as a person.

Consider this excerpt from Zen Master Takuan Soho's famous essay, *The Unfettered Mind*, to Fencing Master Yagu Munenori:

> *...If ten opponents, each with a sword, come slashing their swords at you, if you parry each sword without stopping*

your mind at each action, and you proceed from one attacker to the next, you will not be lacking in a proper action for even one of the ten attackers.

Although your mind acts ten times against ten opponents, if your mind does not stop at even one opponent and you react to the attackers one after another, will you be lacking in proper action?

But if your mind stops before one of these opponent, although you parry his striking sword, when the next man comes, right action will have slipped away from you.

Considering that the Thousand-Armed Goddess Kannon has one thousand arms on its one body, if the mind stops at the arm holding a bow, the other 999 arms will be useless. It is only because Kannon's mind is not detained at one arm that all of her other arms are useful...

Takuan's statements refer specifically to the mental state required for multiple person combat. However, in the broader context, Takuan is also referring to the ideal every day state of mind cultivated by the practice of Zen. By extension, this can be taken to also describe the state of mind of martial arts teachers; whether they are in combat, teaching, or just doing everyday activities.

Lonely at the Top

Harry S. Truman was the 33rd president of the United States. One of the enduring mementoes of his approach to management was a sign on his desk that said:

The buck stops here.

This was a reference to the older saying in 1940s America:

Passing the buck.

Earlier sayings used the term "buck" as a reference for trading with deer skins or passing the dealer's token around a card table. Now it more commonly refers to the one dollar bill and the term "passing" referred to the circulation of currency. As a modern metaphor it is used to describe the passing off of responsibility and accountability, such that it gets lost across a chain of people.

Truman's desk sign was a reminder to himself and his visitors that he was the ultimate decision maker regarding the matters of state that were presented to him.

Martial arts teachers need to have the same attitude. This does not apply so much to assistant teachers, but to the head instructors who have ultimate responsibility for the safety, advancement, and development of all of the students who train at a particular school.

It is very likely that even the chief instructor of a martial arts school has some more senior "master teacher" that they are accountable to for purposes of higher level rank advancement in their particular martial arts style. It is also likely that any martial arts teacher has a number of more senior teachers of the same style who have more advanced technical mastery of that style's body of knowledge. However, the fact that those "masters" exist in no way dilutes or subordinates the accountability of the chief instructor to the students.

The most important decisions in a martial arts school rest with its chief instructor. The chief instructor at a martial arts school will respect the perspectives, mentoring, and coaching of other more senior martial artists, because the chief instructor wants to be a better teacher; not because the other more senior martial artists are the boss. The chief instructor at a martial art school can not delegate responsibility upwards. The buck stops with the chief instructor.

Likewise, the chief instructor has probably delegated many responsibilities to one or more assistant instructors or senior students. However, while responsibilities can be delegated downward by the chief instructor, accountability can not. Being responsible for something means taking the assignment to do it. Being accountable for something means being answerable for the good or bad results and how those results came about.

It is important for martial arts teachers who are assisting chief instructors to understand this and work with their chief instructor in a supportive and communicative manner. Those assistants who have assumed delegated responsibilities must not only execute their tasks effectively, but they must provide the feedback so that the chief instructor can truly be accountable.

The tone for this is set by the chief instructor. It is part of the chief instructor's job to see that the assistant instructors and senior students understand this responsibility/accountability system.

Chi - Ki - Spirit

Martial arts have traditions of cultivating and calling on inner power. In Chinese and Japanese martial arts, the term *Chi* or *Ki* is sometimes used. These terms even appear in the names of some martial art styles, e.g. *Tai-Chi*, *Aikido*, *Hapkido*, etc. Irrespective of the term *Chi* or *Ki* appearing in the name of any particular martial arts style, the concept is universal across most martial arts styles and deserves some attention by martial arts teachers. The Japanese character that is used to represent the term *Ki* is:

The original symbolism of the character is that it represents steam vapors (气), arising from rice being cooked (米) and indicates the idea of spirit or unseen force. The character is used to indicate an invisible, spiritual energy, breath, or life force.

For purposes of this discussion, the English term *spirit* will be substituted for the oriental terms Chi (Chinese) or Ki (Japanese).

When a novice student or non-martial artist looks at advanced martial arts demonstration, sometimes they can not comprehend what they see, based on their everyday understanding. They may observe techniques which appear to defy that common understanding of human capability.

- *How can those black belts break those large blocks of ice with just their hands? Everyone knows that ice is very strong and hard. Everyone knows that even a conditioned human hand is still just made of flesh and bone.*

- *How can that little old guy easily move that great big attacker all over the mat? Everyone knows that the advantage of size can only be overcome with tremendous speed and strength, not with casual everyday movements.*

People have different mental models in that they use to help them shape their world view and make sense of their lives. Often a person with more intelligence and sophistication might use models that are more complex. Likewise, a person with more experience and maturity may use models that are more complete. In any situation, peoples' mental models of how they expect the world to behave always fall short at some point.

At the simplest and most basic level are thought models that describe principles to help people find rational consistency in the everyday things around them. For example:

The whole is always equal to the sum of the parts.

People learn to apply this model in childhood, about the time that they learn to perform simple arithmetic. In adulthood, people apply this thinking continuously and it is an essential requirement for independent living. For example:

- Any combinations of $1, $5, and $10 currency notes that add up to $20 are as good as a $20 bill.

- The bill-of-materials determines the value of the finished item. So the base price of the car, plus the price of all of the selected features determines the list price.

- The caloric load of a hamburger is the sum of the caloric value of the bun, meat, and all of the dressings.

This model of thinking happens so often in daily life and works so well for so many things that often people forget that it does not explain the whole world. From a mathematical perspective this model works very well because many things that humans deal with maintain a relatively constant value over time and maintain a linear relationship with other objects.

Now consider a few common situations where this is not true. When faced with an old-fashioned, coin operated, parking meter, having a one dollar bill is not the same as four 25 cent coins because the old machine takes only coins, not paper currency.

Another situation is when a product becomes obsolete. At that point its total market value may in fact be less that the salvage or scrap value of its individual parts.

Take another example. If a 3 minute song could be purchased as a whole for a $1 download charge, would many people pay $0.33 to download just 1 minute of the song? Would people be willing to pay anything to download just a song fragment? In this situation, the combination of each third of the performance into a whole creates an aesthetic value that is significantly more than the additive value of the three parts.

These are more complex ways of viewing the world because they are based on non-linear behaviors and context changes over time. Other types of conceptual models are needed to understand these examples and other complex real world events like weather and climate changes or stock market behavior. This type of thinking is the realm of people who can adjust and prosper through change: artists, inventors, entrepreneurs, scientists, etc. However, it is also found in any person who has the ability to see things differently and connect unusual patterns.

In the world of martial arts, teachers would probably agree that martial arts performance, as a whole, is not just the simple arithmetic calculation of age, rank, size, and some other easily measurable factors. In martial arts, this gap between the sum of the parts and the whole is explained by spirit. In some sports, such as baseball it might be referred to as *heart*. In other contexts, it might be called *grit*, but for this discussion the term *spirit* will be used.

Spirit can be regarded as a kind of X-factor, an extra something that can be inserted to balance the equation so that the whole can once again be seen as the sum of the part in people's minds. For example:

- *Those black belts were able to break those large blocks of ice with just their hands because they had strong **spirit**.*

- *That little old guy had strong **spirit** and could easily move that great big attacker all over the mat.*

That may sound better, but it did not really explain anything other than to note that these examples are some kind of exception to the rule. It merely created a *leap of faith* or a *suspension of belief*. The idea of strong spirit simply became easier to accept because it helped reconcile, but not explain, the unbalanced equation about martial arts performance. The underlying reason that the mental equation was unbalanced is because common knowledge about martial arts is incomplete.

Of course it is expected that a non-martial artist's common knowledge may be insufficient to truly understand many aspects of the martial arts. So, in many situations it is sufficient to simply say that the missing ingredient that makes impossible things happen is *spirit* and then move on.

The situation is very different when instead of talking about the average person, the subject shifts to the martial arts student. It is important that martial arts students not be lead into a misplaced sense of causality. Martial arts students can experience this problem when acceptance happens in advance of understanding. Consider olden days when a warrior may have well understood that his performance in an approaching battle depended in part on his spirit. In those earlier times, some warriors associated this with metaphysical causality. As a result, the warrior may have turned to prayers, sacrificial offerings, amulets, and other metaphysical devices in order to gain a martial advantage. Also, in earlier times some martial arts had a religious context and martial arts study was part of the training discipline at some monasteries so it was even more culturally appropriate to behave in this way.

In contemporary America, martial arts teachers don't teach metaphysics and aside from some isolated exceptions, martial arts schools in the U.S. are purely secular. However, martial arts teachers should realize that there are psychological and sociological aspects of spirit that influence martial arts performance and behavior in a non-linear way.

To better understand this, consider these common uses of the word spirit.

- *The **spirit** of Christmas Future confronted Ebenezer Scrooge.*
- *The **spirit** of the great president seemed to permeate the Lincoln Memorial.*
- *Aunt Molly was a reformed alcoholic and no longer imbibed in **spirits**.*
- *Our high school class of 2010 had the best school **spirit**.*
- *His competitive **spirit** makes him the most aggressive wrestler on the team.*

In these everyday examples, the term spirit is referring to something that is ephemeral, but still has a concrete effect, even if that effect is transmitted via the mind.

In martial arts there are two major tangible aspects to the concept of *spirit* and both are derived from self-control.

- *The mind controls the body*
- *The mind is relaxed, coordinated, and attentive*

The first aspect of spirit in the martial arts is that the mind controls the body. This principle is simply the application of will power by applying the conscious mind to control the body. By developing their will power, martial arts students can over time engage in progressively arduous training.

Certainly martial artists who can not control their own bodies are very unlikely to be able to control any opponent. In martial arts, some of the common terms associated with the mind controlling the body include:

- Discipline
- Persistence
- Endeavor
- Doggedness
- Tenacity
- Indefatigability
- Perseverance

In martial arts, the concept of the mind controlling the body is not some magical belief in mind-over-matter. There is no intention of overcoming the laws of physics. Instead, this is a consistent and compelling desire by martial artists to better understand and master the physical assets present in their own bodies. It is the role of the martial arts teacher to help the martial arts student overcome their pre-conceived notions of their physical limitations. These pre-conceived notions are often the result of ignorance, ingrained habits, fear of failure, and laziness. As a result they are suitable targets for coaching by the martial arts teacher.

The second aspect of spirit in the martial arts is that the mind is relaxed, coordinated, and attentive. The notion of the mind needing to be *coordinated* may seem a strange concept because in western civilization, people often consider the mind to be a single thing. Earlier western philosophers did not have the benefit of any more than the most superficial knowledge of neurophysiology. As a result, they tried to come up with models that explained the mind in terms of their world view, focusing on considerations of topics like morality (e.g., good vs. evil) and theology (e.g., the soul). As a result, the common culture does not have a terminology to explain the workings of the mind in day-to-day terms. For many contemporary Americans, their notion of the mind, if they have one at all, is restricted to their conscious mind. Even then, they might even be more restrictive and focus on only that portion of the mind that deals with the world using human language (i.e., the cognitive portion of the mind used to read this book.)

For purpose of this discussion, it is not necessary to have a deep understanding of the anatomy and physiology of the human nervous and endocrine systems. It is sufficient to understand that the ability to perform martial arts involves different parts of our body, exchanging information with each other. This exchange of information is not always a simple exchange. It is typically an arbitration, where one piece of information is considered important because of another piece of information coming from a different source. Once a piece of information is determined to be significant, the way subsequent information is processed may be temporarily altered. This information arbitration process involves the cooperation of multiple body organs and systems - even different organs within the brain. There is even some pre-processing of information that happens along the nerve pathways as that information makes its way to the brain.

For the most part people are preoccupied with their conscious mind. However, the conscious mind is only effective when it works productively with the unconscious mind. A simple example of this is teaching a child to catch a ball. Initially, the child will consciously try to copy the movements of the teacher. Then over time, the child can catch without any conscious thought. In fact, the presence of too much conscious thought might be a distraction that interferes with catching the ball.

The same thing happens in martial arts. For example when martial arts students are first taught to strike with a sword, their actions are very much in their conscious mind as they deliberately attempt to imitate the movements of the martial arts teacher. Then, over time and with sufficient practice, the martial arts students are able to strike without conscious thought.

This does not necessarily mean that martial artists are some kind of robotic killing machines that will reactively strike without a conscious decision to do so. It does means that, for the martial artist, the conscious mind and the unconscious mind are working in harmony. The conscious mind is the master of strategy, for example determining the target and the type of strike. It is analogous to a football quarterback calling a play. The unconscious portions of the mind then compute the range, speed, and direction of the martial artist and the opponent and then command the martial artist's body parts to perform their respective work in a coordinated way. At some point in the process, the conscious mind of the martial artist stays out of the way so as not to distract the other parts of the mind and to focus on its job of calling the next play.

It is also worth noting that the interplay between the conscious and unconscious parts of the mind is not uni-directional. Pre-conscious awareness is a crucial martial arts skill. It is important that the conscious mind does not get so preoccupied in thought, that it becomes insensitive to subtle input from the unconscious parts of the nervous system.

Another example of a relaxed, coordinated, and attentive mind is in the area of emotions and how the human nervous system and endocrine systems work together. Hormones trigger physiological changes in the body. Some of these changes alter the mind's perception of the current situation. For example, consider the common hormones listed in the table below.

Gland	Hormone	Function
Adrenal Cortex	Cortisol	Stress
Adrenal Medulla	Epinephrine	Fight or Flight
Adrenal Medulla	Norepinephrine	Blood Pressure

Table 7: Hormones Related to Conflict Situations

These particular hormones are related to stress situations that might be applicable to some martial arts contexts. Increased levels of these hormones will have an impact on both the body and the mind. For example, gross motor skills may be temporarily enhanced, but fine motor skills may be compromised. Likewise, sensory perceptions and judgments will be altered as well. The release of these hormones is determined both by the unconscious and conscious mind. For example, a loud sound might trigger the unconscious mind to order a spike in hormone production. However, this can also be caused by the conscious mind when it perceives, or even just imagines, a hostile, dangerous, or unpleasant situation. When the conscious mind becomes overactive because it is attached to stress related images on a recurring basis, then the conditions exist for various stress related problems, including:

- Heart disease
- Asthma
- Obesity
- Diabetes
- Headaches
- Depression and anxiety
- Gastrointestinal problems
- Alzheimer's disease
- Accelerated aging
- Premature death

Applications of this principle of the mind being relaxed, coordinated, and attentive can be seen outside of the martial arts. In sports, such as golf and tennis, the same concept is referred to as the *Inner Game*. The concept is also found in top level performance for sports like archery, target shooting, and billiards.

The purpose here is not to explain contemporary theories of psychology, physiology, and sports science. Neither is it to suggest that martial arts teachers need to be neurophysiologists. This chapter is about reinforcing these points:

- The "secret sauce" in martial arts training is this concept of *spirit*.
- The application of *spirit* within the martial arts follows two general principles:
  o *The mind controls the body*
  o *The mind is relaxed, coordinated, and attentive*
- Contemporary common knowledge does not provide the martial arts student with an adequate background or vocabulary to easily develop these skills without directive coaching by the martial arts teacher.
- The underlying dynamics of spirit are not religious or metaphysical, but rather based on human physiology and psychology.

- While the underlying science is still evolving, enough is known for martial arts teachers to proceed with a fact-based approach.
- The way that the martial arts teacher will approach this is dependent on their martial arts style and personal experience.

When a martial arts student learns some techniques to take out an opponent, it has very little applicability to every day life in modern society. However, when a martial arts student develops the state of mind (i.e., *spirit*) necessary to learn and execute a technique to take out an opponent, then that martial arts student has accomplished something highly relevant to daily life.

From the perspective of *"the mind controls the body"* the martial arts students will learn that by application of *spirit*, they can control their bodies and accomplish things that they might not have previously considered possible. They will also come to understand that if they can do this in the martial arts, then they can apply that principle to other aspects of their life to accomplish new goals.

From the perspective of *"the mind is relaxed, coordinated, and attentive"* the martial arts students will learn that by application of *spirit*, they can control their emotions and be responsive to changes in their current situation. They will also come to understand that if they can do this in the martial arts, then they can apply that principle to other aspects of their life to calm their spirits and dynamically respond to changing situations.

Reconciliation with Violence

> *...Men, this stuff that some sources sling around about America wanting out of this war, not wanting to fight, is a crock of bullshit. Americans love to fight, traditionally. All real Americans love the sting and clash of battle. You are here today for three reasons. First, because you are here to defend your homes and your loved ones. Second, you are here for your own self respect, because you would not want to be anywhere else. Third, you are here because you are real men and all real men like to fight...*

Speech to the U.S. Third Army (June 5, 1944) - General George Patton

It is too easy to dismiss the famous general's remarks as merely being characteristic of his flamboyant persona. The fact remains that Americans do have a love/hate relationship with violence. America had a violent birth and a violent history. Back in the turbulent 1960s, the radical activist H. Rap Brown had this to say when challenged about the violent leanings of the radical left:

Violence is as American as cherry pie.

Just how violent is the U.S. currently? Consider the following statistics about violence in the U.S.:

Type of Crime	Rate per 100K People
Murder	5
Forcible Rape	29
Robbery	133
Aggravated Assault	263
Total Violent Crime	430

Table 8: U.S. Department of Justice / FBI, "Crime in the United States," September 2010

Having an approximately 1 in 250 chance of being a violent crime victim may not sound so bad. However, that statistic is only for one year. Over the course of 40 years, the statistical accumulative probability rises to a less comfortable probability of about 15%.

Now consider a focus on women in the U.S. According to U.S. Center for Disease Control (CDC) report called, *The National Intimate Partner and Sexual Violence Survey (NISVS)*:

- 1.3 million women were raped during the year preceding the survey.

- Nearly 1 in 5 women have been raped in their lifetime while 1 in 71 men have been raped in their lifetime.
- 1 in 6 women have been stalked during their lifetime. 1 in 19 men have experienced stalking in their lifetime.
- 1 in 4 women have been the victim of severe physical violence by an intimate partner while 1 in 7 men experienced severe physical violence by an intimate partner.
- 81% of women who experienced rape, stalking or physical violence by an intimate partner reported significant short or long term impacts related to the violence experienced in this relationship such as Post-Traumatic Stress Disorder (PTSD) symptoms and injury while 35% of men report such impacts of their experiences.

Now focus on just the veteran segment of the population. Here are some findings in the FBI Bulletin: *The Returning Military Veteran: Is Your Organization Ready?*

- Upward of 35 percent of returning troops may experience mental health issues, such as major depression and generalized anxiety, and seek help for such problems through military programs.
- Common factors leading to increased psychological stress in soldiers include encountering roadside bombs, improvised explosive devices (IEDs), and suicide bombers; handling human remains; killing an enemy; seeing fellow soldiers and friends dead or injured; and experiencing helplessness (e.g., an inability to stop violent situations).
- Unlike physical wounds of war, these conditions—although they affect mood, thoughts, and behavior—usually remain invisible to other service personnel, family members, and society in general; they often go unrecognized and unacknowledged.
- Further, more than 26 percent of troops who have served in combat may suffer from post-traumatic stress disorder (PTSD), an anxiety condition that can develop after direct or indirect exposure to a terrifying event or ordeal in which someone inflicted or threatened grave bodily harm.

Lastly, this focus on school children based on these statistics from the National Education Association (NEA):

- 1 in 7 Students in Grades K-12 is either a bully or a victim of bullying.
- 56% of students have personally witnessed some type of bullying at school.

- 15% of all school absenteeism is directly related to fears of being bullied at school.
- 71% of students report incidents of bullying as a problem at their school.
- 1 out of 20 students has seen a student with a gun at school.
- 282,000 students are physically attacked in secondary schools each month.

The U.S. also has institutional violence. For example, the U.S. has the highest incarceration rate in the world at about 3/4 of a percent of the population. 97% of the offenders in jail today will be released and then return to the communities from which they came and half of those will be incarcerated again within three years.

Americans have an ongoing and almost endless debate about institutionalized violence. It covers topics from capital punishment, to police violence, to racial profiling, to the rights of private citizens to use violence in self-defense, to all types of considerations around the interpretation of the 2nd Amendment. In the post 9-11 era, those debates have expanded to include considerations on the use of pre-emptive warfare, torture, and robotic assassinations by drones and other computerized devices.

Apart from the public debate over the actual risk of violence in America and the corresponding right to resort to violence in response, there is another important aspect of violence. That is the American fascination with proxy violence. The American consumer's appetite for "action" and other related genre of violent entertainment has spawned multiple major industries: movies, TV, Internet, sports, gaming, and even pornography. Some viewers prefer the sanitized depiction of violence, where the byproducts and consequences of violence are not graphically depicted. Other viewers prefer to see their proxy violence accompanied with a gratuitous display of associated gore. There is a concern that "life imitates art" and that the American consumption of proxy violence through entertainment sources may desensitize people to violence or even actually encourage real violence. So far the social science response has been that it does, but it cannot determine when, how much, and under what real world conditions. So it remains a complicated social issue which will receive more study over the years.

Summing up the story of violence in American for a martial arts teacher, the lessons are that violence in America is pervasive, persistent and multifaceted. In order to effectively teach their students, martial arts teachers must come to personal terms with the nature of the violence in their lives and their communities.

Violence happens across every demographic segment of society. Even if a martial arts teacher is able, though circumstance and skill, to avoid ever being in a violent encounter, the overwhelming statistical probability is that the teacher's immediate family, close friends, and students will not share that same good fortune.

Violence in America is an integral part of both America's history and its present. Recounts of violence are very emotionally charged. Sometimes the depictions of past violence in the U.S. are glorified or villainized. Sometimes those depictions get exaggerated or repressed. The important consideration is that it does not matter what Americans want to remember about past violence, or think about contemporary violence, or hope/fear about future violence. American violence has been around since the beginning, and violence is here to stay. It is simply an unpleasant, but critically important, fact of life. As American society has advanced there have been many social improvements which have mitigated violence, but these changes have not eliminated it. It is simply a fact of life in America and one that a martial arts teacher cannot afford to forget.

The underlying dynamics, root causes, and best deterrence of violence have been the focus of countless studies by multiple organizations and numerous experts. This includes work by prestigious organizations like the World Health Organization, the U.S. Center for Disease Control, and the U.S. Department of Justice. Martial arts teachers must realize that there are not simple answers to the questions of violence in America. More importantly, when teaching their students about violence, a martial arts teacher must have the knowledge, confidence, and ego strength to be comfortable as subject matter experts in an area where the absolute answers will remain unknown for the foreseeable future.

Given these characteristics of violence in America, there are four areas of focus for martial arts instructors to consider in order for them to reconcile themselves and teach effectively. These are:

- Understand the civil and socially acceptable and appropriate responses to violence in contemporary American society and specifically in their community.
- Help the students think through the issues of violence in American society as it relates to their own lives.
- Understand how to manage the control of violence in martial arts training specifically as practiced in their martial arts style and school.
- Understand the personal reaction to violence as it occurs in themselves and their students.

It is essential that martial arts teachers understand both the specific regulations in their local jurisdiction and the general societal principles for the application of self-defense. For example, the martial arts teacher needs to know basic practicalities. For example: Is it legal, in their locality, for their martial arts students to transport martial arts weapons between home and the martial arts school? Also, since the martial arts students will be traveling across various local jurisdictions and state lines, they need to have a general understanding of the common principles around the use of force. Many people and even some martial arts students still believe urban myths like:

> *"A boxer's hands must be registered as lethal weapons."*
> *"A martial arts practitioner must verbally declare that they know martial arts before defending themselves."*

The martial arts teacher is not expected to be a lawyer or give legal advice. However, martial arts teachers are expected to be subject matter experts in matters related to the practical applications of martial arts within the context of society.

The core of the current American thinking about self-defense is based on two principles:

- *Stand Your Ground* –focuses on the fundamental right to violent response
- *Duty to Retreat* – focuses on the responsibilities to attempt to de-escalate a potentially violent confrontation

Both principles are relevant to the martial arts.

The *Stand Your Ground* principle holds that a person, who is not engaged in an unlawful activity and is in any place where he or she has the right to be, is justified in using physical violence, including deadly physical force, and has no duty to retreat in when presented with a reasonable fear of imminent death or great bodily harm.

Notice that this principle is based on the defender's inherently subjective perception of both the immediacy and severity of the perceived risk. In examining the legitimacy of a *stand your ground* justification, authorities will often attempt to test a defender's subjective justification for violent defense to see that it was not an overreaction. One basic way of examining this is by applying the "reasonable person" test:

> *What would a reasonable person in the same situation have concluded?*

The *Duty to Retreat* principle takes the position that a civilized person has the responsibility to first avoid violent conflict. If that is not possible, then there is a responsibility to take reasonable steps to retreat; thereby demonstrating an intention not to fight before eventually resorting to the use of force.

This principle focuses more on observable actions of the defender, rather than their perception and state of mind. However, it is not without its own subjectivity. For example, when would it be acceptable to meet the retreat requirement by moving across the room vs. out of the room vs. out of the building?

Naturally people differ with regard to these perspectives and, in the United States, the legal definitions of self-defense varies from state to state. Since it is likely that martial arts students, like most people in the U.S., will be traveling across state lines from time to time, martial arts teachers may not want to spend too much time delving into the idiosyncrasies of their local jurisdiction. However the common American understanding is that self-defense must be:

- **Proportional** – The degree of physical force used in the self-defense act must be appropriate to the seriousness of the situation.
- **Non-retroactive** – After the threat is removed, the self-defense context is ended. Otherwise it is a matter of getting even, taking revenge, or obtaining retribution.
- **Non-preemptive** – Until a threat is imminent, there is no context for justifying physical force.

Sometimes these concepts are extended in a few special cases where a reasonable observer's actions may be conditioned by some atypical past experiences. Examples of this might include *battered women's syndrome* and *post traumatic stress syndrome*, but those issues are beyond the scope of this discussion. Basically, martial arts teachers need to familiarize themselves and focus their teaching on the more general concepts of applying violence for self-defense.

As persons of responsibility, martial arts teachers must be conscious that our society has evolved to the point where there are disclosure expectations when there is even a suspicion of violence related to children. This societal value presents martial arts teachers with potential ethical considerations, even in jurisdictions where they might not technically be compelled by statute to report violence, neglect, or abuse of children.

Beyond the aspect of violence as it related to criminal law, the martial arts teacher must have some understanding of civil law. Actions which may or may not have a criminal consequence may, in fact, carry a significant monetary consequence as a result of civil law liability. The real world is not a zombie apocalypse movie where the amount of justifiable violence has no limits. Martial arts teachers owe it to their students to create an awareness of the potential after effects of the application of the techniques they are being taught.

Nothing prevents the martial arts teacher from occasionally inviting in a lawyer or police official to talk about the local ordinances around violence and the allowable responses to violence. In fact, it is a good idea to do so from time to time if the appropriate resource is available. Primarily, the martial arts teacher is expected to be a lay subject matter expert on the subject of violence and the appropriate responses. Unlike a lawyer, the martial arts teacher can present a much broader perspective, related to the development of martial arts over centuries. Of course it is critical that the martial arts teacher impresses upon the student that the historical perspective will not absolve them from potential criminal prosecution or civil suit if they do not conform to contemporary standards of response to violence.

It really does not matter what a martial arts teacher's opinions are about any of the contemporary issues are related to violence. A martial arts teacher's political views or societal theories are largely unimportant. A martial arts teacher may be a proponent of capital punishment or be for abolishing it. The martial arts teacher may be for broad 2nd Amendment rights or narrow 2nd Amendment rights. The martial arts teacher may lean towards *stand your ground* or *duty to retreat* legislation.

Unlike the olden days of Confucius, contemporary martial arts instructors are not called upon to be experts in social theories or legislative/judicial positions. What is more important than the answers to these complex questions is that the martial arts teacher is an example and a mentor to help students think through the questions and reach their own conclusions. For example, when a student voices an opinion about a topic related to the use of force, the martial arts teacher has a teaching opportunity. The martial arts teacher can ask the student to explain why they feel the way they do and how they came to form that opinion. Then the martial arts teacher can probe for important things like:

- Is this really the student's heartfelt position, or is the student parroting the martial arts teacher's or some other authority figure's opinion?
- Does the student's point of view take into account the whole body of factual evidence that exists or just those facts that support one conclusion?
- Has the student considered various sides of the problem or perhaps tried to identify new points of view?
- Has the student looked at the indirect consequences associated with their position on the topic?
- Is the student's point of view consistent with other aspects of the student's value system as previously articulated by the student?

While martial arts teachers may have strong personal beliefs about societal issues, it is not important that the martial arts teachers expound their social-political point of views. It is certainly not desirable that martial arts teachers exert their leadership positions to influence their students to those views. What is important is that martial arts teachers help their students to be both informed and deliberative in matters related to violence and society. These are not matters where everyone is of the same mind. In situations like these, where people of sound reason may reach different conclusions, it is imperative that martial arts teachers help their students develop an informed/searching approach, rather than a confrontational and dogmatic approach to these issues.

Martial arts teachers should be informed about the leading edge research concerning violent attacks: who is at risk, under what situations, what tactics are used, what are the warning signs, what defenses work best, etc. That requires an ongoing commitment to learning and an open mind. Many martial arts styles were originally derived for combat scenarios which may not resemble today's most common self-defense risks. The teacher will want to have a good understand of how long it takes a beginning student to become competent at basic self-defense vs. how long it takes the student to become a competent practitioner of their martial art style. If there is a protracted period of time where the beginning student is not adequately competent to protect themselves from the statistically likely forms of attack, martial arts teachers should consider how they want to adapt their curriculum to address that gap.

At their very core, martial arts are essentially systems for dealing with violence; both dispensing it and responding to it. In contemporary America, there are some martial arts derivatives that use martial art techniques exclusively for exercise, sport, or entertainment and largely bypass the concept of violence as it relates to martial arts. However, in most martial art styles, controlled violence is a basic underlying component. The substitution of controlled violence for raw violence applies physical and mental controls to make martial arts training safe and sane. It is analogous between the controlled nuclear fission in an atomic power reactor and the uncontrolled nuclear fission in an atomic bomb.

There are two aspects to controlling violence in martial arts:
- Manage physical contact
- Simulate mental intent

Martial arts styles typically employ four methods to manage the potential violence associated with physical contact in training:
- Safety Equipment
- Substitution of techniques
- Prioritization of training
- Contextualization around the encounter

Safety equipment has been around for hundreds of years. For example, it was easy to see that practice with a metal sword or spear had the disadvantage that one could not learn from their own mistakes because those mistakes would be fatal. As a result wooden training weapons came into use. Now, technology enables a wide range of safety equipment for various types of martial art training situations. This includes gloves, footwear, protective padding, and practice weapons. The good side of training equipment is that they let techniques be practiced with more speed and force than one could safely do without the equipment. The down side of safety equipment is that it changes the dynamics of the martial situation. For example, a real sword will cut through a person while a wooden sword will stop when it contacts a person. (This principle was well illustrated in the dueling scene in Akira Kurosawa's famous movie *Seven Samurai*.) In training a student to use a sword, it is desirable for them to get a sense of the sword passing through their opponent. As a result the martial arts teacher must balance the different methods of practice so that the idiosyncrasies of the training weapons do not dominate the student's approach to the art. Similar principles apply to unarmed training as well. In disciplines outside of the martial arts, this phenomenon is sometimes called *Risk Compensation*.

Risk Compensation is what occurs when people adjust their behavior in response to the perceived level of risk, behaving less cautiously where they feel more protected. In this situation, the use of safety equipment can create a pattern where the martial arts student develops less safe habits because of reliance on the protective equipment.

It should be remembered that while some safety equipment may resemble armor, safety equipment is not a defensive weapon. During periods where armor was in use, martial arts styles developed many techniques for leveraging and countering the use of defensive weapons, including armor. In modern times, safety equipment is largely used transparently and martial arts techniques do not leverage or counter them.

Substitution of techniques can be seen in many martial arts training situations. Often this is accomplished by simply moving participants further apart, substituting far for near, so that they are just outside of the striking range or just on the border of physical contact. Another common adjustment is to change the speed of the techniques used in partner practice, substituting slow for fast, so that there is simply less force in any physical contact. Sometimes a nearby non-vital target is substituted for a vital target on the body, thereby keeping certain areas of the body "off limits" as targets. Finally, the techniques themselves may be substituted with less dangerous techniques that utilize similar body movements. For example, a technique which might be applied against the movement of an opponent's joint is replaced with a technique that moves in the same bending direction of the opponent's joint. In another case, an eye gouge technique may be replaced with a palm strike to the face. The theory behind all of these substitutions is that if the martial arts student develops the control to execute their moves safely, they will have no problem applying the more dangerous move if there was a real life need.

Of course this approach also has a down side, the student may have a tendency to condition themselves to the safety rules and expose themselves to openings that cannot be exploited in the training situation. Likewise, the student who always practices within the comfort zone of these safety rules may not be prepared for either the physical or mental intensity presented by the truly violent intent of a real attacker. The martial arts teacher has the responsibility to impress upon the students the differences between the training situation and the outside world. Otherwise, martial arts training can actually make a martial arts student more vulnerable in a violent encounter.

Sometimes violence in martial arts training is controlled by the prioritization of how training time is allocated across different aspects of training session. Martial arts classes contain a variety of activities: conditioning exercises, breathing and meditation exercises, solo forms, two person forms, free sparring, etc. The mix of activities varies with the martial arts style and the particular school. The martial arts teacher may adjust the time allocated to different aspects of martial arts practice to minimize the exposure of the student to potential violence during the class. This adjustment may also take into consideration the experience level of the student. For example, in many martial arts styles, beginning students either spend less time sparring or have additional safety constraints placed on them when they are sparring.

Whenever students are training in martial arts, it is essential that they maintain an awareness of context. In other types of physical training it may be acceptable to "zone out". Some runners may like to listen to music on their headphones while running. Health club members may like to watch TV will working on the treadmill, stationary bicycle, or stair machine. That approach may be fine for some activities, but it is hazardous for martial arts training. In martial arts training it is important for students to always be context aware, martially alert, in touch with their surroundings, mindful, etc.

One of the reasons that martial arts emphasize formal politeness is respect. However, another reason is that the practice of formal politeness is a training technique to build a habit of contextual awareness. By practicing politeness, martial arts students are acknowledging the arrival or departure of a person, sometimes themselves, from a particular context or situation. By doing that, the students are practicing awareness of their context. The same principle applies to the practice of technique. If the martial arts student can not control their mind, they will have difficulty practicing safely when they are working with a partner.

One of the main tasks of the martial arts teacher is to help the martial arts students maintain the correct mental focus throughout each training class. Depending on the particular style and school, that focus may be more edgy or relaxed. However, even if it is edgy or it should not be paranoid or rigid; even if it relaxed, it should not be casual or sloppy. The martial arts student's focus needs to be set to the martial context that the martial arts teacher is trying to create for that particular training session.

Martial arts teachers need to understand the dynamics of violence at a personal level. Real violence carries with it an intention to do harm that can only be simulated in martial arts training. This violent intention may be emotion filled and fuelled by anger, rage, hate, or desperation. It is also possible that the violent intent can be "business" rather then "personal" and have little emotional context; what is sometimes referred to as "stone cold" or "cold blooded". Either way, a violent encounter brings with it a potentially powerful intention to do great bodily harm. From the perspective of game theory the rationale behind it is straightforward. An overwhelming show of force can overcome an opponent without exposing the attacker to the personal risks of a full give-and-take fighting encounter. In recent U.S. military history, this tactic was called *shock and awe*. It is also a key principle in police arrest techniques. This strategy also has a down side. In those situations where it does not work, it can lead to a cycle of progressively escalating violence. Since the initiator stepped up the initial violence to a high level, the responder will, if given the opportunity often try to up the response to a higher level of violence.

In martial arts training, simulation is used to acclimate the students to violent intentions. There are three training techniques employed to simulate violent intentions:

- **Martial Scenarios:** This is the mental role playing that goes on during the practice of kata, sparring, or just about any activity during a martial art class. In the beginning, this might just mean that the students are asked to imagine an attacker standing there as they learn to practice a punch. Over time, the martial arts student's eyes become trained to look for any tactical mistake, vulnerability, or opportunity and their responses become quick enough to exploit them.
- **Intensity / Commitment:** Presumably all of the students in the class are friendly and collegial. When working as partners, it can be difficult for students to stay focused because they do not perceive any harmful intention from the person whom they know well and were chatting pleasantly with a few minutes ago. It is therefore important that the martial arts students who are playing the role of the attacker perform their assigned function with intensity and commitment. The simulated attacker must fully consume the defender's attention so that the defender can learn properly. The simulated attackers may not have violent intentions, but they must have a level of intensity and commitment at a level that is the same as if they did.
- **Physical Consequences:** At its heart, martial arts are not academic pursuits. Martial arts do involve a good deal of learning that is cerebral; this book would be an example. However, much of the learning that needs to happen is visceral in nature and happens with what is commonly called "muscle memory". For example, repeated verbal reminders to martial arts students to keep their guard up are corrections without consequences. However, getting knocked down because of a low guard is a lesson instantly learned because getting knocked down is an appropriate consequence for dropping one's guard. In a violent situation, the amount of force used to accomplish

the knock down might be destructive and cause injury. It might also place the defender in a disadvantaged situation where protection from the follow-up attack was not possible. Naturally, the martial arts teacher will want to simulate the consequence enough to create the learning situation, but not so much that there is physical injury. This type of correction is seen in weapon practice. If a martial arts student gets rapped on the hand with a wooden practice weapon, they may respond with "Ouch!", their partner may respond with "I'm sorry.", and the martial arts student will likely reply "No. It was own my fault." The martial arts student realizes that the discomfort of having one's hand rapped is a self-correcting consequence of having one's hand in the wrong place.

Martial arts teachers need probe the depth of their own hearts and help their students to do the same. Certainly martial arts teachers are typically not psychologists anymore than they are lawyers. However martial arts teachers must understand that:

- Violence is traumatic, not just to the body, but to the mind.
- The human psychological effects of past violence persist into the future, even across future generations.
- A violent encounter effects both the aggressor and the defender; the perpetrator and the victim.
- Violent encounters release brain chemicals that enhance both the immediate and long-term effects of a violent encounter. This impacts both the conscious mind and also the more primitive unconscious areas of the brain.
- Violence creates a mindset that may not be readily reconcilable with everyday life going forward because the latent memory distorts the view of normalcy and creates uncertainty around everyday matters of trust and safety.

The martial arts teacher must be able to deal with the real world experiences of the student with respect to violence. A student that has been impacted by violence will be transformed by it. However, even a student without a history of violence-induced trauma will still have an uneven reaction to the simulated intent of violence that is used in martial art classes. The propensity to violence is an essential human trait. This propensity toward violence carries both adaptive and dysfunctional characteristics as regards to civilized living and the evolution of the human species. Society's pervasive ambiguity regarding the legitimate role of violence is an essential conflict that has been at the heart of many fairy tales, literary themes, and philosophical discussions. For the purposes of this discussion, assume:

- An inborn propensity to violence which has a normal statistical distribution (i.e., it is strong for a few, weak for a few, and somewhere in the middle for most people.)

- A socialization process which either constrains or inflames the natural propensity.

For a person growing up in a war zone, it might be very adaptive to be quick to personally engage in violence as basic survival strategy. On the contrary, a person growing up in a very "civilized" and orderly society would have more of an incentive to distance themselves from personally disruptive and threatening behavior. In both cases the mathematics is the same. What is different is the inflection point on the curve where selfish individual aggressiveness and the ability to achieve more by being a trustworthy member of a group meet.

Consider martial arts students who either have a tendency to be needlessly rough or a hesitancy regarding close practice with their partners. Both situations can be indicators of past experiences with violence or, more likely, just the student's reaction to the recognition of their own innate propensity toward violence. As martial arts students work through the routine of practicing with their partners, their minds bring up associations with real or imaginary past experiences of violence.

At one extreme, a martial arts student may tap into their primal rage. To a martial arts beginner, this appearance of violent intent in their opponent may appear to be very intimidating. However, an experienced martial artist will quickly see through it and realize that such ferocity is a dead end (often literally.) The overload of angry aggression deadens the martial arts student's senses and makes the student unable to adapt to change-ups in the situation. So while a visceral berserker approach may be good preparation for suicide shock troopers (they are expendable) or the Incredible Hulk comic book figure (he is virtually invulnerable and does not exist anyway), it does not have a place in high-level martial practice. Furthermore, it obscures the correct path forward for lower level martial arts students. Martial arts teachers who encourage their students down this path may want to revisit the *Karate Kid* movies and see exactly where exactly the Cobra Kai went wrong.

On the other extreme is the martial arts student who is intimidated by any mental visualization of violence and simulation of violent intent. To a non-martial artist, such a tendency may seem to be a virtuous position. After all, what right-minded person would not be repelled by violence? However, that point of view embraces a false dichotomy and is codependent. First of all martial artists cannot protect themselves from that which they cannot understand. Unless martial artists can confront the issue of violence without blinking, they becomes, or remains, a prisoner of violence.

There is also the matter that at some deeper level, the extreme aversion to violence is not so much a fear of being the subject of violence as much as it is a fear of being subjugated by violence. This would include the fear of awakening the inherent propensity to violence that is within each person. This

119

kind of fear and aversion will ultimately manifest itself in the martial arts students' techniques. It is another fatal flaw. Of course, the martial arts teacher can not simply tell their student to "toughen up" and "get over it." The martial arts teacher must work with the student to grow past their deepest fears.

Ultimately as martial artists gain experience, they acquire more choices in how they respond to a situation. Attachments, either positive or negative to violence, inhibit the options that a martial artist has in the moment of an encounter. This is why in martial arts there is not a matter of denying or embracing violence. It is more a matter of accepting violence and reconciling it.

Martial arts students are not immune to rape, robbery, mugging or other violent acts of aggression. Their physical encounters will not always be successful. Neither are martial arts students always able to respond to violence in a measured and appropriate way. The martial arts teacher needs to be prepared to deal with all of these situations.

The martial arts teacher is not a therapist. However, martial arts teachers can help their students to control their minds and learn to be in the present, even when they are confronted with emotionally charged memory associations. This is the true value of martial arts training. Martial arts student cannot change their past, but with dedicated training they can discipline their minds so that they are no longer hostages to their past.

The martial arts school is, in the most basic sense, a workshop of violence, yet for the students who train there, it must also be a sanctuary from violence. The balancing act is the responsibility of the martial arts teacher. To the extent that martial arts teachers are not themselves reconciled with violence, they will not be able to help their students to do the same.

Reconciliation with Death

> *...The Way of the Samurai is found in death. When it comes to either/or, there is only the immediate choice of death. This is not particularly difficult. However, you must be determined in advance. Claiming that to die without reaching one's objective is a dog's death is the frivolous rationalization of sophisticates. When pressed with the choice of life or death, it is not necessary to achieve one's objective. We all want to live. And in large part we rationalize our decisions according to what we like. But not having attained our objective and continuing to live is cowardice. This is a thin dangerous line. To die without gaining one's objective may be a dog's death and viewed as fanaticism. But there is no shame in this. This is the substance of the Way of the Samurai. If by setting one's heart right every morning and evening, one is able to live as though his body were already dead, then through sacrifice one achieves freedom in the Way. His whole life will be without blame, and he will succeed in his calling....*

Hagakure: Book of the Samurai - Yamamoto Tsunetomo

The samurai, Yamamoto Tsunetomo, captured many aspects of Bushido that modern martial arts teachers would consider to be outdated. Simply put, the world view of Imperial Japan had a self-centered arrogance which eventually helped fire the cause of Japanese expansionism leading up to the epic violence of WWII.

In contemporary American society there is an ambiguity and a raging social debate about the "sanctity of life". The debate is not about some abstract notion of life being precious, but rather the contemporary debate is about the practical application of the principle in everyday situations and the underlying meanings of the words *sanctity* and *life*.

Old Japanese notions such as ritual suicide just do not get the traction in the U.S. that they did in Japan. The different world views of the two cultures lead to different expressions of values in this area of life and death. In the U.S., the common culture, rightly or wrongly, considers a focus on death as a dysfunctionality. Cultural prohibitions draw a thin and faded line between self-sacrifice and suicide. Notions of death acceptance are colored by the Freudian construct of a death wish (i.e., Thanatos) and the news media stories of mass murder and suicides triggered by depression and psychotic despair by social outcasts.

In western thought, historical events like Thermopylae, Masada, and the Alamo as well as classical heroic stories like the Roman Horatius Cocles at the

Tiber river bridge, or the Swiss Arnold von Winkelried at the battle of Sempach, are merely relegated to anecdotal footnotes in history.

However, Tsunetomo's message only narrowly applies to suicide, more broadly it applies to non-attachment to self. When looked at from that perspective it becomes much more comprehensible to the contemporary American mind. It is even possible to see similar points raised in western European thought as seen in the Christian synoptic gospels:

> ... Whoever wants to be my disciple must deny themselves and take up their cross and follow me. For whoever wants to save their life will lose it, but whoever loses their life for me and for my teachings will save it. What good is it for someone to gain the whole world, yet forfeit their soul?...

Matthew 16:24-26 / Mark 8:34-36/ Luke 9:23-25

To put this in a martial arts perspective, it is important to understand the state of mind that martial arts training seeks to cultivate.

There is a difference between confidence and resolve. Confidence is the willingness to rely on what is thought or hoped to be true. A martial artist may feel secure in their speed, strength, strategy, and technical skills. This is important, but it can also be arrogant. In a fight, anything can go wrong. Also, any comparison with an opponent's capabilities is opinionated and subject to error.

A novice at the martial arts might like to think that their weapon or their technique is what protects their life from their attacker. This is superficially true, but ultimately, that kind of confidence is a false hope. An advanced martial artist knows that the attacker's weapon can easily become the defender's weapon. The reverse is also true. It also applies to any attack, not just a weapon. Every attack becomes a potential opening.

So, while confidence is a good thing, it is not absolute and may be inflated. Ultimately, confidence may be as self-defeating as a lack of confidence. Resoluteness is different from confidence. It is a commitment to do something without regard to adverse consequences.

Resoluteness, combined with non-attachment to self is the generalized concept behind Tsunetomo's remarks. It is also an important theme in Musashi's book.

> ...*Generally speaking, the Way of the warrior is resolute acceptance of death. Although not only warriors but priests, women, peasants and lowlier folk have been known to die readily in the cause of duty or out of*

122

> *shame, this is a different thing. The warrior is different in that studying the Way of strategy is based on overcoming men...*
>
> <u>A Book of Five Rings,</u> Miyamoto Musashi

Of course this kind of resolute mindset requires great mental and spiritual strength. This is one reason why meditation has traditionally been considered a core part of martial arts training.

An illustration of this principle can be seen in the following story:

Tokugawa Iyemitsu, the Japanese Shogun, had a pet monkey. The monkey was very quick and would dash about the court creating all kinds of mischief. One day the Shogun Iyemitsu had enough of the monkey's insolence and issued a challenge for his samurai retainers. "You retainers are the leading warriors of the land," he proclaimed. "See if any of you can match your speed and martial skills against my monkey and teach him a lesson."

All of the samurai tried their best, first trying to catch the monkey and then just trying to hit it with a stick. However, the monkey was just too fast and agile; running all around the Shogun's court, alternately hiding behind the Shogun's chair and darting out again.

Even the great master swordsman, Yagyu Munenori, joined the chase, but was not able to touch the Shogun's monkey.

It happened that Takuan Osho, the Zen Master, also was attending the Shogun's court that day. Finally, after he had become disenchanted with the lack of samurai success, Shogun Iyemitsu, now already in ill humor, became even more irritated when he looked over at Master Takuan's placid expression. So the Shogun defiantly extended his monkey challenge to Zen Master Takuan. Without hesitation, Master Takuan got up, approached the monkey, and brandished his monk's staff. Instead of running away, the monkey immediately cowered submissively before him.

Shogun Iyemitsu was astonished. "How is it that a Zen monk could accomplish what Japan's leading warriors could not?" asked the Shogun.

"That is simple." replied Master Takuan. "All of the samurai were afraid of accidentally hitting you as they chased after the monkey. The monkey was able to perceive this and use it to his

advantage by alternately running behind you as you sat on the dais. However, when I approached the monkey, he realized that I did not care at all if I struck you."

This story is interesting because the monk outperforms the martial artists. Although they were trained and pledged to give up their lives at a moment's notice, the warriors could not overcome their awe of their leader and as a result lost their resolve for the task at hand. Meanwhile the monk was not only unconcerned by the status of the shogun, he was not distracted by the possibility of a death sentence for striking the Shogun. The monk was both resolved and non-attached to self.

The story also has a lesson to martial arts teachers. Just as the monkey in the story was able to perceive the monk's intention, martial arts students are likewise perceptive and are subliminally influenced by their teacher's state of mind. It is therefore important that the martial arts teacher always be reconciled with death.

Always Fresh; Always Final

> *Today is a good day to die.*

Attributed to Tasunka Witko A.K.A. Crazy Horse. Possibly
derived from the Lakota Sioux war cry *Nake nula wauŋ welo*!
(I am ready for whatever comes).

American culture has seen a variety of popular religious and secular self-help books focusing on the topic of *living in the moment*. The topic has been around for centuries, in one form or another, in both eastern and western schools of philosophy. While the topic has been a successful area for contemporary U.S. book sales, it is difficult to perceive how much of an overall grip it has on contemporary American identity. It would seem in today's America is a culture where the more dominant philosophy is consumerism, fueled by commercialism. This propels American society for in an insatiable quest aimed at future consumption. When looking at the political identity of contemporary America, there seems to be little ability for society and government to focus collaboratively on the problems of the present. In the U.S. there appears to be a much greater desire to indulge in speculative ideological debates on the intentions of the founding generations of politicians or to look fearfully into an uncertain future.

Martial arts practice is an inherently existential pursuit and has a unique ability to help its practitioners understand the value of living in the moment. Just as an atomic cyclotron can create miniature conditions that validate the physics of large cosmic events, the physical techniques in martial arts are a laboratory that gives their practitioners brief glimpses into the tangible value of being in the moment. By learning the value of being in the present while executing a technique, hopefully martial artists also see the value in extending the exercise to other parts of their lives. In addition, many martial artists cross train in meditation and other complementary disciplines which help to make this transference that takes a spark of awareness from a technique and kindles it into a different way of living life in general.

As a group, martial artists may be more inclined to consider the value of living in the now than the general public. The general public may not be so clearly aware of the specifics of this exercise. However, within the common perception of martial arts is the notion that martial artists have somehow honed their senses and reflexes to some sharper focus. Of course, an enhanced ability to sense and respond may be a secondary consequence of living in the moment, but it is not at the core.

It is the role of the martial arts teacher to step up as a role model to help new students acquire a correct insight into this existential phenomenon. Martial arts teachers should not only practice living in the moment, but they should be a demonstrable example of life in the moment.

Of course living in the present is a large topic and there are many ways to approach it. Some approaches are more suitable for certain people and certain circumstances. With respect to martial arts teachers, here is one exercise that is specific to their unique role:

> *Teach every class as if it were the student's first class.*
> *Teach every class as if it were the student's last class.*

The implication of the first statement is not to make assumptions about the student coming in for training. Martial arts teachers should not let past familiarity lead them to take for granted a student's capabilities or experience. When a student steps on the mat, the martial arts teacher's perception should be fresh as if they were meeting for the first time. Martial arts teachers must constantly strive to make each training session a once-in-a-lifetime proving ground for the student.

The implication of the second statement is that each class should be the martial arts teacher's final gift to their students. Martial arts teachers should teach each class as if they have only this one last chance to make a difference in the life of each student. This is not a call for drama. While life changes can occasionally be dramatic, more often they are small, open, honest, and very much tuned to the situation of the moment.

This is what is meant by saying that martial arts teaching should always be fresh and final.

Section 3 – Passing It Forward

Everyone interacts and influences other people. It happens in families, work places, and in a wide variety of community and social settings. Teachers are unique among most people because they have, by definition, a broader and explicit mission to interact and influence other people.

The martial arts teacher has the opportunity, if not a responsibility, to pass on a rich and valuable legacy that ideally results in changed lives and self-realized individuals.

Of course, this implies that martial arts teachers must be self-realized themselves, aware of their capabilities and desiring to pass on more than a bag of martial arts tricks.

Consider the following story about a martial artist attempting to find his identity as a teacher.

> *Shoju Ronin, the Zen Master, was approached by a samurai who was looking for advice. Introducing himself to Master Ronin, the samurai explained his problem.*
>
> *"Ever since my youth," began the samurai. "I have been disciplining myself through the study of swordsmanship. For over 20 years, I had trained in a number of different fencing schools until I had mastered all of their secrets. I now have a great desire to establish a school of my own and I have been devoting a great amount of work to making this happen. My problem is this. In spite of my best efforts, I have not been able to articulate the true essence of my school...Something that would clearly distinguish it from all others. Is it possible for you to teach me a way to find it?"*
>
> *After listening very attentively, Master Ronin stood up and walked over to where the samurai was sitting. Master Ronin then proceeded to hit the samurai three times very hard and kick him such that that the samurai toppled over onto the floor. The rough treatment caused the samurai to have a sudden enlightenment and instantly have new insight into his fencing art.*

Zen Stories of the Samurai, Neal Dunnigan

This last section of the book focuses on some considerations for martial arts teachers as they consider their future legacy. Unfortunately, most martial arts teachers are not set up for an explosive breakthrough from Master Ronin and must commit themselves to a protracted effort to plot their course.

The Role of Teacher in Society

The early teachers who brought martial arts from Asia to America faced many difficulties, but they also had an edge. Coming to a new culture and being a martial art missionary/evangelist was no picnic. However, Asian culture provided them with one advantage: a sense of entitlement to respect.

In Asian cultures, *respect* is a pervasive, traditional, cultural value. It was formalized, promoted, and refined by Confucianism. Even in the People's Republic of China, where in the 1960s the Cultural Revolution proclaimed that "Confucianism is Dead!", there are still pervasive Confucian cultural values, albeit they are now tempered by free market egalitarianism.

Perhaps it was self-serving on the part of Confucius, but in his philosophy of social responsibility where he outlines the social contract between different strata of society, Confucius was able to retain a prestigious place for teacher/consultants like himself. As a result, the vocation of teaching in the Asian world is one that is respected and if not monetarily enriching, is none the less always held in high esteem.

In the Western world, social philosophers like Nicholai Machiavelli, John Locke, Karl Marx and others also wrote extensively about the social contract, but their sharing of their world views did not elevate the position of the teacher/consultant in western society as Confucius did in the east.

So when the martial art missionaries came to the U.S. from Asia they had a certain advantage from the mystique of being from another culture. They expected their students to adhere to the respect for them and their teaching as they would in their own country. Over time they succeeded because they were able to attract students who conformed to those values. On the negative side, sometimes this leads to students who were unquestioning or tolerant of dysfunctional behavior on the part of the foreign martial arts teacher.

When American martial arts teachers try to arbitrarily mimic this kind of socially reinforced authority, they find that it just does not work. The comedic expression of this is presented in the movie *Napoleon Dynamite* where the "Rex-Kwon-Do" teacher is pummeling his students with expressions like **"BOW TO YOUR SENSEI!"** In American culture, the students will expect an American teacher to behave and express him or herself like an American.

American martial arts teachers can expect to be held to a higher standard than the martial arts teachers from whom they may have learned. Many martial arts students will not closely listen to broken English and a thick accent. Many martial arts students will expect instruction to be clear and easily rationalized. This is all part of the evolutionary process of America internalizing martial arts and making them native, rather than foreign to American culture.

One problem for the American martial arts teacher is that the role of "teacher" in American society is not as respected as it is in other cultures. Americans like to view themselves as a people characterized by *action* rather than *contemplation*. Consider the American expression:

> *Those who can't do, teach.*

It is a long and involved story that is beyond the scope of this book, but as a profession, teaching in the United States tends to receive nominal, rather than genuine respect.

Back in America's pioneer times, townspeople would compensate a teacher primarily by providing room and board. Teachers were expected to take lodging with an assigned family and remain under close social scrutiny. They were forbidden to get married and expected to stay celibate. It was not necessary to get the best teaching talent in exchange for providing a proper livelihood; often it was simply to get the cheapest deal for the community.

In contemporary America, there is a populist trend of generalized antagonism toward government at all levels and civil service of any kind. This includes teachers who are perceived as having guaranteed government jobs, good benefit plans, and living off of the public tax base.

Perhaps the major exception has been America's immigrant communities. Traditionally these groups have seen education as a gateway to opportunity and realization of the American dream. As a result these groups have often had a higher regard for education and teachers. However, as various immigrant groups are mainstreamed, it is not apparent that they necessarily maintain these values across generations or spread them to the mainstream culture.

One may certainly argue that this should not be the case; however, it is more difficult to argue against the prevalence of such points of view in the American society at large. Of course any one individual teacher may still be a hero to his or her students or their families and their communities. Unfortunately, the exception does not generally influence the perception of the whole profession.

Another consideration is that the general public has little appreciation, and therefore little respect for personal accomplishments that require the commitment of years of sustained effort. In popular culture, *talent* is more associated with *aptitude* then it is with *practice* and as a result, there is a lack of awareness and recognition of the dedication required to master an art. The advances in technology have devalued the need for manual dexterity across the whole of society. Professions and trades which required skilled use of hands and which took years to master have been radically changed by the introduction of computerized machinery. Since progressively fewer people have personally experienced the kind of multi-year commitment required to master an art or skilled trade, it is difficult for people to even be aware of or value the effort involved in such sustained endeavors. Therefore there is not an automatic respect of mastery based on years of effort.

The result of this is that prospective students are not likely to have consistently studied and trained at any one thing. Neither are they apt to have close personal friends who have. So the notion that the martial arts teacher has a rare level of skill based on years of effort and that this should merit an automatic level of respect is foreign to them. In contemporary America, it is often simply outside the previous experience of prospective students and their support system. It is only after they fully engage in their own martial art training that they begin to understand the disciplined struggle required to acquire skills and then develop a better understanding and respect for others who have already gone through similar training experiences.

Martial arts teachers need to be aware of the cultural attitudes that students bring with them when they come to class. Accordingly, the martial arts teachers need to accept that students and students' families will tend to initially undervalue the instruction that the martial arts teacher has to offer.

In contemporary America the student is often viewed as a consumer. As such, the key factor in the teacher/student relationship is that respect is based on value, rather than role-based status. This understanding is an important key to successfully teaching martial arts in contemporary America.

The martial arts teachers must fundamentally understand and be able to share their understanding of:

- The value of martial arts in society
- The personal value of studying and practicing martial arts

This type of communication fosters trust and creates earned respect. It lets the martial arts students see their commitment of time and effort as a personal investment. It lets martial arts students view their martial arts teachers as trusted advisers as well as experts in their subjects.

It also differentiates the teacher-student relationship in martial arts as being fundamentally different from a grade school or college teacher-student relationship. The teacher-student relationship in martial arts is not about a single semester or a single subject. Rather it is about sustained guidance down a path of a life and death struggle with oneself.

It is important that martial arts teachers understand the underlying past experiences and assumptions that their students have about the teacher-student relationship. Where these reinforce the teaching of martial arts, they should be embraced and leveraged. However, where the contemporary American perspective is not conducive to the teaching of martial arts, then the martial arts teacher must work to differentiate their role from the more common notions of what a teacher is in contemporary America.

From Teacher to Master Teacher

> *...Spare no effort when you teach. You advance as your students advance. Do not be impatient when you teach. No one can learn everything well at one time. Perseverance is important in teaching as are patience, kindness, and the ability to put yourself in your students' place...*

12 *Rules for Aikido Instructors*, <u>Aikido in Daily Life</u> by K. Tohei, 10th Dan

> *...It is almost unavoidable that any training method or system tends to become fixed and mechanical...There needs to be strength, knowledge, experience and insight from the side of the person who presents this system, i.e. the teacher who is capable of transcending its limitations...*

Test Guidelines for Instructors, by T.K Chiba, Aikido Shihan

Japanese martial arts from the feudal period used the old system of *menkyo* or *certificates of proficiency* to track the progress of students and teachers. In modern times, Professor Kano, the founder of Judo was instrumental in popularizing the modern kyu/dan (white belt/black belt) grading system to track the progress of martial arts students. Kano's kyu/dan system has been adopted in some form by many martial art systems; both Japanese and non-Japanese. The fact that the contemporary American culture does have a general awareness of some progression in martial arts through a succession of colored belts and then a succession of "degrees" of black belt is a tribute to the success of Professor Kano's kyu/dan system.

Outside of the martial community, people have less awareness that there are different, but related paths in martial arts for technical advancement and teaching advancement. Some family members and friends of martial arts students may even be aware of a subtle differentiation of terms like "teacher", "master", or "grand master". These titles refer to a hierarchical classification based on different levels of teaching skills.

In many martial art systems, technical advancement through the kyu/dan belt system and teaching advancement are different, but related systems. The reasoning behind this is that if martial arts students have no interest in teaching, they should still have the ability to progress technically. In the case of non-teaching martial artists, their progress is more individual and focused on how well they can master the syllabus of techniques in their style of martial arts. In the case of the martial arts teacher, it is a given that they have some mastery of their style's syllabus. The differentiator is that martial arts teachers are also distinguished by how well they can engage students in the learning process and how effectively they can transmit what they know to others.

Many of the topics in this book describe things that teachers need to do or be aware of in order to instruct martial arts effectively. Taking those topics into consideration, it is clear that at some point in a practitioner's martial art advancement, teaching can be a great help for the personal development of that practitioner as a martial artist. However, teaching is not for everyone. A martial artist may be focused on some narrow goal of technical perfection and not have the time and energy for teaching. For example, competitive martial artists do not have much time to devote to teaching when they are training for upper level tournaments. Other martial artists do not have the motivation, aptitude, or temperament and may be skipped from rotation when it comes to opportunities to lead a class. Finally, some more advanced martial artists may only want to dip their toe into teaching and are willing to assist, but do not feel called to take on full scale teaching responsibilities.

While it does not apply exactly the same to all martial arts, there is a common progression for a teacher that typically advances through three levels.

- *Associate Teacher*
- *Journeyman Teacher*
- *Master Teacher*

The first level is that of *Associate Teacher*. This is a person who has been recognized by the leadership of their martial arts style as having the interest and aptitude to teach and has demonstrated a corresponding technical competency by performing at a black belt level in that style. At this level the martial arts teacher is expected to teach the same technical content that they have been taught, following the same pedagogy that was used to teach it to them. The focus for these beginning level teachers is on following the established forms.

Of course there is a whole world of other teaching skills that are likely not included in the curriculum and pedagogy of a martial art style. For example, it is not typical for martial arts teacher formation programs to formally specify the dynamics of all of the interactions between teachers and students or teachers and the extended community of prospective students and student support systems. These are skills that the lower level teacher should be learning on their own, through observation, and by seeking the mentoring of more senior martial arts teachers.

In most martial arts systems, this *Associate Teacher* would be expected to already have achieved a lower level of black belt; depending on the style, somewhere between 1st and 4rd degree.

In U.S. K-12 public education, the equivalent of the Associate martial arts teacher can be thought of as a teacher who has graduated with a bachelor's (i.e., 4 year college) degree and has obtained a provisional teaching license.

In a larger martial arts school, *Associate Teachers* may be *assistant teachers*. When a martial arts school is big enough where it offers more classes than the chief instructor can personally teach, and some students have advanced enough to reach the black belt level, those senior students may be at the point where they help the chief instructor with some of the teaching tasks, perhaps even taking on-going responsibilities for teaching certain classes. In martial arts schools an *assistant teacher* is often an *auxiliary teacher* in the sense that they are a proxy instructor for the classes when the chief instructor is not available. In that situation, the chief instructor of the school is still responsible for:

- The personal relationship to the student and tracking of the student's training, problems, and advancement.
- The direct supervision and development of those associate/assistant instructors in that school.

In other situations, the *Associate Teacher* may, in fact, already be a chief instructor of their own school. In this situation, there is no concept of being an "assistant"; the *Associate Teacher* has full responsibility for school administration, the teaching program, and long-term student development. This kind of *Associate Teacher* may only have limited certification to transmit the more advanced teaching of their martial arts style. That is not nearly so important as the fact that they have the final responsibility for the development of the students under their charge. This *Associate Teacher* is not just conducting classes and instructing techniques, they have exclusive personal ownership of the on-going teacher-student relationship.

This kind of *Associate Teacher* is not under any type of day-to-day supervision. However, often there is still some process, directed by the leadership of their martial arts style, for periodic mentoring and developing *Associate Teachers*, so as to bring them to the next level of teacher development. Typically, this means that the *Associate Teacher* has some restrictions and development obligations. The *Associate Teacher* typically has limits on the level of promotion that they can autonomously give to their students. Also, the associate instructor may be expected to conform to some on-going advanced training and mentoring, for example: attending a certain number of advanced seminars, or providing status reports on their development progress.

The Second level is that of *Journeyman Teacher*. *Journeyman* is an old term for someone who is fully accomplished at their particular trade. For example, it would be expected that a journeyman plumber, electrician, carpenter, mason, can independently handle any construction problem involving pipes, electricity, wood, or stone respectively.

In martial arts, a teacher at this level is not just teaching what they have been shown; they are teaching what they know. This is a subtle, but important distinction. The *Associate Teacher* is focused on following form. Forms, conventions, and patterns are ways of making activities more effective by systematizing them. This is like baking a cake from a cake mix. It still tastes good, but the process for making the cake has been simplified. Using a mix frees the cake baker from needing to know the specific characteristics of all of the individual ingredients and their unique behaviors during different parts of the cake making process. The *Journeyman Teacher* is still making the same cake as the *Associate Teacher*. However, the *Journeyman Teacher* is working from understanding, not simply forms, conventions, and patterns. The *Journeyman Teacher* can actually make the same cake from scratch and where necessary substitute one ingredient for another.

This additional insight into how the techniques work enables the *Journeyman Teacher* to bring additional teaching tools to the class. At this level, the martial arts teacher understands, and can recognize, all of the common mistakes made in the execution of the techniques. In addition, the *Journeyman Teacher* will have insight into a large number of exercises to deconstruct and correct a student's technique.

In the modern U.S. K-12 public education system, this would be analogous to a teacher with a maser's degree and a full teaching certificate.

By this time, the teacher would have been expected to have gained additional technical mastery of their style and reached the 3rd through 6th degree level of black belt or its equivalent.

The *Journeyman Teacher* is expected to be able to operate autonomously with respect to their students. At this higher level the martial arts teachers have fewer limitations on promoting their students and typically have less structured official requirements regarding their own mentoring and advancement. At this level, the *Journeyman Teacher* may also begin to develop some capabilities around teaching martial artists how to teach martial arts. *Journeyman Teacher* may be grooming some of their students to become teacher-tracked themselves. They may also be mentoring other *Associate Teachers* in other schools.

The third level is that of *Master Teacher*. The *Master Teacher* is recognized by the leadership of their martial art style as being able to transmit the entirety of their martial art style without error. Typically, the *Master Teacher* has reached a level of technical skill at or above the 6th degree level of black belt or equivalent. By this time they are likely to have had multiple decades of experience in their martial art style.

This top level of teaching authority has few restrictions on it and the *Master Teacher* has few limits on promoting students and little supervision by the leadership of their martial art style. In fact, at this level a martial arts teacher is in the leadership of their martial arts style.

A significant characteristic of the *Master Teacher* is that they not only have a full mastery of the martial arts style, they also have a mastery of the pedagogy for transmitting it. For example, *Master Teachers* will not only know a given technique and its relevance in the curriculum, but they will also know how to instruct other teachers to teach it more effectively. In this way, a *Master Teacher* is also a *teacher of teachers*. They are not only a leader among their peers, but actively seek to raise the level of leadership across all members of their peer group. By way of analogy, it is like a college professor with a doctoral degree in education who trains the bachelor and master degree students to be teachers.

Across different martial arts styles, these teaching levels may be known by various names. For example, some Japanese martial arts styles may refer to these levels as *fukushidoin*, *shidoin*, and *shihan*. Other Japanese martial art styles use different terminology like *renshi*, *koyshi*, and *hanshi*. There are a wide variety of titles and terminologies used across different martial arts styles. Different martial arts styles can also have more or even fewer teaching levels. However, it is common in martial arts styles for the leadership to recognize different levels of teaching capability and associate the progressively higher levels with more autonomy and authority with respect to the transmission of that particular style of martial arts.

These formal development programs vary tremendously in approach and thoroughness across various martial arts styles. The models for martial arts teacher training programs can vary from boot camps, to resident apprentice programs, to continuing education programs. Often, these formal organizational certification processes may have a primary focus on the teacher's ability to accurately transmit that particular martial arts style. Of course that is important, but it is only a part of what teaching martial arts is about.

To some degree, these formal teacher certification processes are more apt to recognize progress in a teacher's development than they are to create progress in a teacher. For example, some levels of certification may require attending a certain number of clinics, seminars, and camps. This kind of advanced training is important for a martial arts teacher's development, but at the higher levels, these training events do not create a proportional increase in the martial arts teacher's knowledge of teaching. To a greater extent, these training events are a demonstration of attitude and passion. The martial arts teacher's participation in these events and the corresponding expenditure of time and expense are an expression of sustained commitment. The willingness to periodically attend training events where the martial arts teacher is now a junior, rather than a senior, is an expression of humility and a desire to learn. So in addition to whatever technical or pedagogical lessons a teacher may have garnered from a teacher training event, what is more significant is that the training event is an opportunity for the martial arts teacher to demonstrate:

- Sustained commitment
- Openness and humility
- Curiosity and a desire for life-long learning

The real progress as a martial arts teacher results from individual initiative and perseverance. Martial arts teachers should have a commitment to continual improvement and must remain at heart a student-for-life. This drive to continuously learn and improve cuts across three dimensions:

- Technical perfection of their martial arts style and the science of teaching
- The relationship between their martial arts style and their life
- The art of teaching itself

To the extent that the teacher has embodied those principles, it is reasonable to expect that that teacher is learning all of the time. Failure to consistently maintain those standards can reduce the potential of ten years of teaching experience to be the equivalent of the same one year of teaching experience ten times over.

The teacher programs that martial arts styles put in place to guide teacher development are both helpful and inherently incomplete. They provide an external reference to measure the martial arts teacher's conformity to the martial art's style and they provide a third-party oversight into the martial arts teacher's progress. However, martial arts teachers are ultimately responsible for their own development as martial artists and teachers. That very sense of responsibility should take martial arts teachers through their own martial art style's teacher training program and beyond.

Legacy

To a large extent, the study of martial arts is an enduring commitment to wrestle with opposites. These include classic paradoxes such as: peace-violence, gentleness-force, calmness-action, confidence-humility, etc.

The same is true from the perspective of teaching martial arts. One of the most pervasive of these is finding the correct mix of preservation vs. innovation.

The repository of martial arts knowledge is largely organized according to martial arts styles and transmitted through martial art schools which are associated through those styles. In this context, tradition brings a lot of value. For example, the specific methods of various martial arts styles have been tested and found to be valuable over many years. Also, within a given martial arts style, the reference point to a common core curriculum makes it easy for martial artists of that style to train together, even if they are from different schools. As a result, martial arts are generally tradition-bound and martial arts teachers are, to a large degree, preservationists in that they are called to preserve the traditions and methods of their style and support the particular organization that promotes it.

Naturally there is another side to this. As martial art styles are transplanted across cultural boundaries or passed to newer generations, certain contextual aspects of the art change. It is also the case that general knowledge about sports physiology, body mechanics, and learning theories continue to advance independently of the martial arts. For these and other reasons, martial arts teachers are also called to be innovators. This means that martial arts teachers constantly call upon their own general life experiences and seek out new life experiences to make their martial arts teaching become more alive and relevant.

There is yet another, more personal, aspect to the preservation vs. innovation dilemma. Consider a basket of kittens. Some kittens will have a more conservative nature and will stay closer to their mother. Other kittens will be more adventurous and wander further from the basket to explore. This propensity to be conservative or adventurous can be seen across many animals, including people. Both extremes have their risks. However, in nature, the existence of both conservative and adventurous members of a species creates a diversity which helps protect the species through both constant and changing times.

The lesson here is that in addition to the greater societal forces that shape the preservation vs. innovation direction of a martial arts style, there are also the innate personality traits of the martial arts teachers that make their temperament conservative or adventurous, and therefore lead them to be more inclined to be preservationists or innovators.

Even beyond that, martial arts teachers will find that their own martial arts students will have their own personal temperaments toward being conservative or adventurous. Over time, this can result in a martial art style that is characterized as being very traditional, giving birth to an offshoot which is very innovative (at the time.) Yet, generations later, that offshoot's teachers may ironically be very set on the path of preservation.

As martial arts teachers think about their legacy and what they are trying to accomplish via their teaching, they need to confront their own personal role as a preservationist or innovator. That choice of where they want to be on the preservation-innovation scale rests solely with them. To some degree, the choice is based on external factors and to some degree, it reflects the martial arts teachers' own personal disposition.

Ultimately, the martial arts teacher must see that this is not simply a matter of compromise between two opposite camps. Rather than pick a midpoint between the two extremes, the martial arts teach must fully embrace both extremes and internally reconcile the differences. By doing that the martial arts teachers will hopefully get to a state where they can develop their own framing of the argument and evolve to their own integrated view of where they need to be.

Whatever choice each martial arts teacher makes, they must remember that their students are watching them and trying to make contextual sense of what they are being taught. So it is important that martial arts teachers be open and clear in communicating their perspective to their students, while realizing that at some point in the future, some of those students will find a need to take things in a different direction.

The Hawthorne Effect

> **Hawthorne Effect:**
> *(A.K.A. "observer effect") is a form of reactivity whereby subjects improve or modify an aspect of their behavior, which is being experimentally measured, in response to the fact that they know that they are being studied, not in response to any particular experimental manipulation.*
>
> Wikipedia

The science of Industrial Engineering had its roots at Northern Electric's Hawthorne manufacturing facility in Illinois. In the 1920s-30s many studies were done at the Hawthorne plant to test the impact of various conditions on manufacturing efficiency. There were no robotics in those days and the manufacturing assembly line's productivity was largely dependent on sustained human effort. Various experiments at the Hawthorne plant included changing the lighting and other environmental conditions in an attempt to elicit enhanced productivity. What the early Industrial Engineers began to observe was that during the experiment, productivity would tend to go up. However, after the experiment, when the targeted changes were implemented, the anticipated productivity improvements did not materialize. By the 1950s, the next generation of Industrial Engineers began to understand that the mystery of the earlier Hawthorne data reflected the psychological impact of having a team of "experts" periodically watching and measuring production on the shop floor.

So what could be the relevance of this Industrial Engineering paradigm to martial arts instruction? Before considering that, first consider how the Hawthorne Effect can be understood in other disciplines, in this case music.

Take the example of a community orchestra or choir that has a guest instructor come in for a special performance. A guest conductor of an orchestra can often encourage to musicians to perform at a higher level than they typically do, simply because the direction style is fresh and piques the musicians' attention without any preconceived notions. After the guest conductor has gone, the home conductor can leverage this referenceable peak performance to create a sustained improvement in the orchestra. This is an example of how the Hawthorne Effect can be used to great advantage in a musical setting.

A similar thing can happen in martial arts. Seminars, camps, tournaments, guest instructors, and other special events are all important parts of the martial arts diversified learning experience. They provide stepping stones for the martial arts student's future independence from the teacher. Observing these opportunities also provides martial arts teachers with feedback that they can then use to improve their own teaching methodologies.

The important thing here is that martial arts teachers need to learn to not be the center of their students' universe. They must not be jealous or want to be the sole focus of their student's learning process. The suggestion here is not that martial arts students should be casual in respecting their teachers. Rather it is part of the martial arts teacher's responsibility is to create new training opportunities for their students. This includes exposing their students to a more diverse set of martial arts training and teachers.

This kind of martial arts diversification has different implications. At the most basic level it is being introduced to new techniques and broadens the martial arts student's personal understanding of the martial context. There is an old saying:

When all you have is a hammer, everything looks like a nail.

The implication here is that a broader vocabulary of techniques helps the student better understand different martial situations. A martial arts teacher might choose to use this to some advantage. For example, a martial arts teacher may choose to focus more class time and attention on basic technique and core training, given the knowledge that the martial arts students will be attending seminars where they will be exposed to other variations.

Another consideration has to do with the martial arts teacher trying to replicate their own learning experience with their own martial arts students. Simply put, there is no cloning methodology in the martial arts. The martial arts teacher's own learning path was full of sequences of events, opportunities, and contexts that are unique and unrepeatable. Even if the martial arts student is being trained in the same martial arts style and learning the same kata, the martial arts teachers' and their students' experience will be different because they have different teachers.

Just consider any martial arts master teacher. That martial arts master teacher may train multiple martial arts teachers who are all certified as competent to carry on the martial arts style. However, no two of them will be the same. They all will have unique personalities and life experiences which will cause them to express their martial arts teaching differently. From this perspective, martial arts teachers are never really just:

Teaching what they have learned.

Rather, they are:

Applying what they have learned to continually evolving teaching situations.

The implication here is that each martial arts student becomes, to some degree, a unique learning experiment. Looking at it this way, martial arts instructors can utilize the Hawthorne experience to their advantage and leverage it beyond simple improvements attributable to novelty. By exposing their martial arts students to a guest instructor, martial arts teachers can observe their student's learning from a different perspective. The guest instructor may show a different aspect of some concept that will cause something to "click" in a martial arts student's mind and raise that student's level of understanding. Or maybe as in the Hawthorne Effect, simply the pressure of attention and inspection will raise the level of a student's performance by some amount. While in the case of the original Northern Electric productivity gains were only ephemeral, the martial arts teachers have the opportunity to make their student's improvements durable.

From Kata to Technique to Art

> *A martial arts kata is a pre-determined set of movements that are performed either alone or with a partner. The movements represent the application of technique in a narrowly defined simulated martial context and provide a repertory of movements that are the kinesthetic vocabulary for a particular martial arts style.*

Pointing at the Moon: Teaching Martial Arts to Change Lives

Notice that in this definition, the movements themselves are not techniques, but rather, they represent techniques. Very often, martial arts teachers do not explicitly make this distinction and simply refer to the movements in the *kata* as techniques. That is perfectly fine for purposes of simplifying the instruction for the student, but it leaves out some important points.

The term *kata* is something that is not well understood, even by many martial artist students. Typically it is translated as the contemporary American English word *form*. Over the past half century, America has changed from a manufacturing society to an information society, and the typical image that is associated with the word *form* has changed. Now, a *form* is commonly considered to be an ordered list of instructions. Examples of this would include: surveys, web forms, job application form, and income tax return forms. However, not too many years ago, people's first image when hearing the word *form* was that it is another word for a *mold*. It was something that you used to change the shape of an object, sometimes by liquefying material and pouring it into the form, and sometimes by applying pressure to bend the object into the shape dictated by the form. Think of a form used for casting or stamping metal, or a form used to pour concrete, or a wire form used for training the shape of a growing bonsai tree, or dental braces, or a form used put a broken leg in traction while it heals.

A martial art kata may be like the more contemporary meaning of *form* in the sense of being an ordered set of instructions. Katas are structured and typically teach a specific sequence of movements. If martial arts studies were merely concerned with the transfer of information, then that level of understanding might be sufficient.

However, it is much more important that the kata be understood and treated like a form in the sense that it transforms student into some new shape. Some of this transformation is literally about the visible shape of the student. For example, kata practice should transform the students' posture and walking gait. This transformation should be visually apparent and carry over into the students every day posture and movement.

Mostly, the changes that come to a martial arts student from kata practice are more subtle. Katas use movements that simulate techniques in order to instill fundamental martial arts principles into the martial arts practitioner. It is the shaping of the student to conform to these principles that make katas important. Different martial arts styles may emphasize different principles in their katas, however some principles are at the core of all martial arts. These include:

- Agility
- Awareness
- Balance
- Calmness
- Concentration
- Coordination
- Flexibility
- Speed
- Perception
- Power
- Timing

Notice that there are multiple relationships between these principles. For example:

- Speed plus Awareness lead to Timing
- Balance plus Timing lead to Coordination
- Flexibility plus Coordination lead to Agility
- Calmness is a catalyst for all of the principles

It is the responsibility of the martial arts teacher to teach kata in such a way that the martial arts student is actually learning principles through the practice of kata. This is a matter of using good coaching techniques as appropriate to that particular martial arts style. To depend on the rote repetition of the kata to properly form the student and ingrain the principles is a haphazard approach to teaching martial arts. It is inappropriate for two reasons. First it is inefficient and does not make the best use of the student's practice time. Second, unguided practice can lead to the ingraining of incorrect principles. It is still important for the student to diligently and repetitively practice kata outside of class. However, during class, the martial arts teacher must challenge the student's progress by monitoring their kata practice and giving appropriate coaching.

In order to succeed with this approach, it is best if both the martial arts teacher and martial arts student recognize that the true purpose of kata practice is change. It is not uncommon for a junior martial arts student to memorize a kata's sequence of movements, be able to perform them without falling over, and then say something to the martial arts teacher along the lines of "OK. Got it. What's next?" The martial arts teacher's role is to guide the student away from superficial technique, i.e., sequence without principles. Movement sequences can be learned from a book or video. The martial arts teacher's unique role is to ensure that the practice of kata is truly transformative.

When observing both beginning and more advanced martial arts students practice the same kata, it is like listening to a beginning music student and an accomplished professional musician play the same simple piece of sheet music. The sheet music is like a kata. It lists a specific sequence of notes to be played. Even if no mistakes are made in playing any of the exact same notes, there are still profound differences in the musicality of the sound of the beginning music student and a accomplished professional musician. The difference is the deliberate and expressive use of pitch, inflection, intonation, volume dynamics, and other musical qualities. These are musical qualities that master musicians develop from years of training and practice.

Earlier it was mentioned that kata movements represent the application of technique in a narrowly defined simulated martial context. When beginning martial arts students are practicing a kata, their interpretation of the kata presumes a fixed martial scenario as defined by the martial arts style and martial arts teacher. This is true for both solo and partner methods of kata practice. The object of the practice for these students is to stay within the box as defined by that one martial scenario. Of course, the students will practice imperfectly and make mistakes. However, at the beginner level, the students are expected to try to continue on along the script of the kata.

By contrast, intermediate students are at the point where their challenge is applying principles, not recalling movement sequences. Their kata practice starts to become more of an exercise of awareness than an exercise in rote memory. At this point, the martial arts teacher may begin to introduce multiple variations into the kata practice. The variations make the intermediate student aware of alternate martial contexts associated with the katas. Over time the intermediate student realizes that the alternate variations relate to dynamic adaptations that the intermediate martial arts students' bodies make as they become sensitive to their application of principles to the kata. At this level, the intermediate martial arts student begins to practice the kata as technique.

The transition from beginner to advanced martial arts student is not like toggling a switch going on. As students advance in the martial arts they will simultaneously have characteristics of a beginner and an intermediate student. For example, when intermediate martial arts students are introduced to a new kata, they must still go through the earlier process of initially practicing it to learn the sequence. They may pass through this more quickly than when they were a beginner. However, it is still present. Even very advanced students will often practice partner kata slowly at first to insure that they have not forgotten the sequence and to adjust to each others movements. Then they will proceed to more advanced execution of the kata.

Ultimately, the advanced martial arts student will go beyond the bounds of kata and kata with technique. The advanced martial arts student will be able to freely and spontaneously apply the principles of their martial art style to any situation. Naturally, this takes a tremendous amount of time, effort, and training by the martial arts student. It also takes work on the part of the martial arts teacher. First of all, the martial arts teacher must foster an appropriate awareness in the mind of the martial arts student that such a level of competency even exists. Without this awareness, the student will be unable to correctly formulate a goal or focus their training. Secondly, the martial arts teacher must coach the student to see the continuity across all of the movements in their martial arts style. When the student begins to appreciate the underlying connections between seemingly different movements and apply them in their practice, then that student is moving toward the practice and expression of an art.

Boxes of Time

Time management consultants will often speak of time as some kind of container, representing a person's time as a finite resource, and the goals that a person wants to accomplish as objects that a person tries to fit into his/her container. Multiple large objects (i.e., goals) may be difficult to fit into the container of time. The large objects also leave gaps between them. These gaps represent unused time. However, when people deconstruct their goals into smaller tasks, those tasks become easier to manage. In this container metaphor, those smaller tasks fit better into the box of time because they can be packed more tightly or wedged into the spaces around larger tasks. Given the right combination of large and small tasks, more can be accomplished in a fixed amount of time and less time will be wasted.

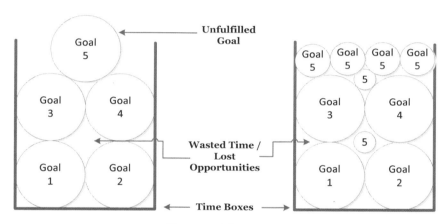

Figure 15: Time Boxes

Certainly those same principles apply to martial arts teaching. There is only a certain amount of time for a martial arts teacher to accomplish what they are trying to do. From the perspective of teaching martial arts, there are at least three goal areas for martial arts teachers:

- *School Development*:   Attract and retain students
- *Student Development*:   Guiding a student to become a mature martial artist/person
- *Personal Development*: Become a better teacher / martial artist / person

In the area of School Development, there are some very different situations. Some martial art schools are operated as not-for-profits and use donated space in a community center or university. The martial arts teacher may receive an honorarium, but does not draw a salary. This model of operations is sometimes referred to as a "club" model. The other end of the spectrum is the fully "commercial model" with owned or rented space, possibly a franchise participant, and a chief instructor with a salary. Typically the "club model" best reflects the operations of small martial arts schools and the "commercial model" better reflects the operations of larger martial arts schools. Certainly, some martial art schools have characteristics of both. For example, some of the larger martial arts schools are incorporated as not-for-profit educational organizations.

There is quite a bit of material, including books, magazines, seminars and consultants that focus on the mechanics of school development. Even martial arts teachers who consider themselves to be traditionalists (i.e., would never offer "Little Ninja Birthday Parties", dress up like a turtle, and let the birthday celebrant cut the cake with a samurai sword), can still benefit from understanding the commercial principles of modern martial arts marketing.

This book does delve into those areas of martial arts marketing. There is only one point to be made here relative to the box of time as it relates to School Development. The smallest integral task, related to School Development, which can be fit into the time box, is the *encounter*. An *encounter* is when the martial arts teacher comes into social contact with a student or a member of the public. The *encounter* may happen in the course of teaching. For example, the martial arts teacher may approach a student and offer a correction. However, more often then not, the *encounter* happens off the mat. In the off the mat situation, the *encounter* could be: greeting a student on the street, becoming introduced to a friend or relative of a student, sending a press release to the newspaper, speaking at the Lions Club or Rotary Club. Even the mundane act of going to the supermarket while wearing a shirt with the school logo is an *encounter*.

It is easy to see that these social interactions / *encounters* by the martial arts teacher are largely analogous to the interpersonal encounters as a martial artist. It is expected that martial artists maintain martial awareness in all of their personal encounters. Likewise, it is also true that for the martial arts teachers, each social encounter is an opportunity for School Development. It is also true that just as martial awareness does not mean that the martial artist is always standing in some fighting stance, encounters with martial arts teachers are not all about recruitment or retention in a superficial or fanatic way. Rather, they are about being connected, positive, and open.

As brief and transient as it is, the martial arts teacher should see each encounter as a once-in-a-lifetime opportunity. This is much like the old saying from Zen Archery:

One Arrow: One Life

Student Development can be looked at in even more detail, as if there were different size objects. Certainly the *encounter* is still the smallest unit, but there are also larger contiguous units related to Student Development that the martial arts teacher deals with.

Perhaps the most important time unit for Student Development is the *class* (i.e., teaching session). An experienced martial arts teacher should have an idea of what each of their students might learn in any given *class*. Hopefully, the martial arts teacher does not just present *class* material because it is what is on the syllabus or scatter that material to the winds like seeds in some primitive form of unattended agriculture. Ideally, the martial arts teacher teaches mindfully, understanding the meaning behind the *class* material and is fully aware of how that relates, at a personal level, to every student's understanding. Even if the martial arts teacher knows that a student will not "get" the material in a particular class, the martial arts teacher is deliberately using the opportunity to bring the student to the point where they will later understand. In those particular class situations, the martial arts teacher is either nurturing a seedling, planting a seed, or even preparing the ground to later plant a seed. Martial arts teaching is indeed a very intensive type of agriculture.

Of course, this kind of individualized attention to each student's immediate apperception is a very high but crucial standard that martial arts teachers should aspire to. It is similar to the kind of concentration and clarity of thought that is needed for a martial artist to face multiple attackers.

This concept was elegantly explained by the 16th century C.E. Zen master, Takuan Soho, in his essay: *The Unfettered Mind*. Takuan used the notion of the 1000 armed goddess/bodhisattva of compassion Kwannon (A.K.A. Guanyin or Guanshiyin) to illustrate how a martial artist could deal with multiple things as long as there was no fixation on any one thing.

There is another time object related to Student Development which is larger than the *encounter* and smaller than the *class*. This is the *activity*. Typically a well orchestrated martial arts *class* integrates all of its *activities* into a unified theme, so the concept of an *activity* is not so important from a time management perspective. However, special notice to the time management of *activities* should be made for youth classes and beginner classes where the attention span of the students is more limited and the concept of a unified theme is less relevant. In these cases the 5-10 minute *activities* become important building blocks of the *class*.

A larger, but still important unit of time for Student Development is the student's *goal*. The *goal* might be to accomplish some specific technique, to win some level of a tournament, or to pass some particular rank test. The martial arts teacher and the student have a shared interest in each *goal*. The student is always responsible for doing the work required to achieve their *goal*. After all, it is the student's *goal*, not the teacher's. However, the martial arts teacher is always accountable for the student's *goals*. The martial arts teacher will first want to see that the student's *goals* are appropriate and well-framed. That is the first part of the martial arts teacher's accountability. The martial arts teacher will then take on the role of a coach/trainer/consultant and see that an appropriate training plan is in place for the student's success. That is the second part of the martial arts teacher's accountability. Naturally, to the extent that the martial arts teacher is unaware of the student's *goals*, the martial arts teacher has no shared interest and is not capable of exercising appropriate accountability.

This concept of shared *goals* is what separates a student's primary teacher from a guest martial arts teacher or any number of assistant martial arts teachers. Typically, only a martial arts school's chief instructor owns the student relationship and has the shared relationship around a student's *goals*. A chief instructor at a martial arts school must be up to the task.

Personal Development refers to the time that martial arts teachers spend on their own advancement as martial artists and teachers. The biggest objects may be *certifications* for teaching or master teaching levels. Somewhat smaller objects may correspond to *master classes* or *teachers' seminars*. The most important objects are quite smaller and correspond to the *encounter* and *class* objects discussed earlier. The most important time object related to Personal Development is the *self-evaluation*.

Whenever martial arts teachers have an *encounter* or conduct a *class*, they must set aside a time for reflection and do a self-evaluation. Martial arts teachers must have a relentless passion for self-evaluation and not let an event pass by without suitable scrutiny. How else can they know that they are on the right track?

Regardless of the goal: School Development, Student Development, Personal Development, or other, martial arts teachers must have a sense of urgency regarding time. If they believe that the martial arts that they teach are of value, then it would follow that martial arts teachers will want to make the absolute best use of their individual boxes of time.

Teachable Moments

One of the greatest distortions of martial arts in the common culture is the misrepresentation of the balance between learning and practice. Like other avocations, such as sports or music, each hour of new learning is backed up by many hours of practice; sometimes hundreds of hours of repetitive practice for each hour of new learning. Of course, depicting such repetition does not make for good entertainment in movies, video games, or performances. Even so, the fact remains that in a typical martial arts class, the martial arts teacher will proportionally spend very little time presenting new material. Most of the time budget of the class will be spent on conditioning exercises, repetitive drills and review of previously introduced material. These are the activities where the martial arts teacher takes on the roles of trainer and coach; they focus on reinforcing and correcting, rather than the presentation of brand new material.

Given that the time budget for presenting new material in a typical martial arts class is relatively small, martial arts teachers need to always be conscious of the readiness of their students to accept new information, so as to maximize the effectiveness of those teachable moments.

This is an area where the traditional approaches of martial arts teaching can be enhanced by understanding more modern theories, drawn from other disciplines, which describe how people learn new skills. This is a broad subject and this chapter will only attempt to touch briefly on one small aspect of it as an example. The example to be briefly considered here is: *Interference Theory*.

Interference Theory is used in education and research psychology to explain some of the obstacles that the human brain encounters when trying to learn new facts or motor skills. In this model, the term *interference* refers to the blocking / inhibiting effect that one set of knowledge and experiences has on another set of knowledge and experiences. There are three scenarios that are used to describe the main learning problems explained by *Interference Theory*:

- *Proactive Inhibition – Old patterns suppress new patterns*
- *Retroactive Inhibition – New patterns suppress old patterns*
- *Latent Inhibition – Old patterns obscure new insights*

Proactive inhibition is a scientific recasting of the old truisms:

> *You can't teach an old dog new tricks.*
> *When all you have is a hammer, everything looks like a nail.*

In *Proactive inhibition* people experience difficulty learning new information or skills because of things they have previously learned. For example, when learning a second language, people may carry over the pronunciation, grammar, and diction of their native language, even though it does not apply to the second language. Likewise a person who has learned to swing a baseball bat or tennis racket may inappropriately carry over some of those movements when learning to swing a golf club. In these situations, the mind is reacting as if these different skills were variants of the same skill, rather then different skills that share some abstract similarities. As a result, the new behavior automatically inherits unrelated and unwanted characteristics of the old behavior.

Usually within a given martial art style, the syllabus is designed so that teaching new material progressively builds upon the earlier material and *proactive inhibition* should not occur. However, students do not typically come to a martial arts teacher as blank slates. Students come into the martial arts with various patterns in their thinking and movements derived from their previous life experiences, perhaps even from other sports or prior martial arts training.

In some previous context, the student may have been correctly taught to **always** keep their feet pointed a certain way or **never** raise their arm above a certain level. Unfortunately, the **always** and **never** aspects of the learning get extended beyond the original context where they were appropriate and they now become a hindrance to adopting new motor skills.

It is also possible that something that was originally intended to be taught as an incidental has become learned by the student as if it were a fundamental. As a result, it gets applied in situations where it is not called for and it interferes with the correct performance of some new skills.

Sometimes a martial arts teacher might "help" a beginner learn a movement by tolerating certain beginner mistakes. Very often martial arts teachers will introduce a new student to a "beginner's way" of executing a basic move or technique. If for some reason, the martial arts teacher does not later go back and correct them, then these errors can become ingrained as bad habits and can become a cause of *proactive inhibition* later on.

In other disciplines outside of *Interference Theory*, these same phenomena might be referred to as *anti-patterns*. In any case, the application of *proactive inhibition* to martial arts teachers is that sometimes it is not sufficient to simply teach something new. Sometimes it is necessary for the student to be deprogrammed or untaught the old material through a sequence of progressive conditioning.

Retroactive Inhibition is a scientific recasting of the old truism:

A new broom sweeps clean.

Retroactive interference is when a person has difficulty recalling old information because of newly learned information. As with *proactive inhibition,* the mind is reacting as if these different skills were variants of the same skill, rather then different skills that share some abstract similarities. In *retroactive interference,* the unique attributes of the new learning get associated with the domain of the earlier learning in such a way that the prior learning is suppressed. This is the situation when a student in history class or Sunday school, associates the attributes of a character they learned about recently onto a character that they learned about earlier. For example:

- *Washington freed the slaves.*
- *Moses took two of each kind of animal into the ark.*

In martial arts, this can often be seen when sequenced behavior is being taught. A martial arts student may have had not problem performing a kata that they already knew, then after being introduced to a new kata, the performance of the old kata begins to degrade. This can particularly be a problem with martial arts students who suffer from dyslexia and have a tendency to inappropriately transpose material across different techniques.

Latent inhibition is a scientific recasting of the old truism:

Familiarity breeds contempt.

The term *latent inhibition* means that it is easier to learn new information and adopt new behaviors when the stimulus is novel rather than routine. When the Russian psychologist Ivan Pavlov was doing his experiments where he conditioned dogs to anticipate a food reward after hearing a bell, he observed a interesting phenomena. Dogs that came from places where they were not previously exposed to bell sounds performed better in the experiments than dog who came from places where bell sounds were common. Novel stimuli have a greater ability to bond with new associations than familiar stimulus. Pavlov was studying the effects of neutral stimuli being used to condition involuntary responses (a.k.a. Classical Conditioning), however, similar effects can be seen in other kinds of more complex behavioral change and learning situations.

Consider the health problems associated with the modern American diet. Many people can eat based on unhealthy food choices on a daily basis, without any immediate ill effects. There is nothing differentially significant in more one potato chip, one more French fry, one more glass of beer, etc. As a result, creating a dietary behavioral change can be very difficult, even if the abstract awareness of significant long-term health risk is intellectually understood.

In the martial arts everyday motions need to take on a martial characteristic in order to properly develop martial awareness. *Latent inhibition* helps explain why this can be a difficult to do this at the reflexive level, even when it is understood at the intellectual level.

Statistical theory suggests that martial arts teachers should expect to see the effects of each type of inhibition follow normal distributions in a large enough class or across multiple classes of martial arts students. In this normal distribution, most students would have some learning impediment from time to time, a few students would never exhibit any problem, and a different few would have recurring problems. So the challenge for martial arts teachers is that the class typically has only one teacher, but the students are a heterogeneous group with different learning capacities, independent of their rank or skill level in their martial art.

If a martial arts teacher wants to seize a teachable moment and reach the majority of the class, the martial arts teacher must be prepared to anticipate any potential impediment to the absorption of the new material. In this example *Interference Theory* was used as an example. However, there can be any number of potential problems that the martial arts teacher should consider.

Depending on the situation, the martial arts teacher may decide to precede the new material with a review of relevant old material. Alternatively, the martial arts teacher may decide to break down the new material into basic skills and teach them in a layered fashion; adding one layer at a time until the full concept is presented. Another possibility is to show the new skill from multiple different contexts, such as how it might be used to defend against different types of kicks and punches. There are many other different approaches that martial arts teachers can use to introduce new material. The key is to match the approach to the learning obstacles that are presented by that particular class of martial arts students at that particular time.

This approach is a departure from certain older training methods, such as expecting the student to *steal the technique* from the teacher, where the burden of learning is disproportionately placed on the student. In those older training methods, the teacher was focused on teaching to the top of the class rather than teaching to the middle of the class. It is important for martial arts teachers to understand when it is their goal to direct their teaching to the top of the class, the middle of the class, or even the bottom of the class.

The martial arts teachers do need to know how to seize the teachable moment. They do not necessarily need to have advanced degrees in physical education, or psychology, but they do need to understand those things that inhibit learning and what to do about them. From that perspective, it can be advantageous for martial arts teachers to look outside of their discipline to see how other disciplines have scoped these problems and what solutions have been proposed that might add value when teaching martial arts.

Teachable Students

> *Whoever corrects a mocker invites insult.*
> *Whoever rebukes a wicked man incurs abuse.*
> *Do not rebuke a mocker or he will hate you.*
>
> *Rebuke a wise man and he will love you.*
> *Instruct a wise man and he will be wiser still.*
> *Teach a righteous man and he will add to his learning.*

Proverbs 9:7-9

There is an old saying that goes:

> *Seeing is believing.*

From the perspective of teaching martial arts, sometimes the converse is more important:

> *Believing is seeing.*

People, in this case martial arts teachers and students, tend to see what they expect to see. In other disciplines, this is sometimes referred to as *Confirmation Bias, Confirmatory Bias,* or *Myside Bias.* Simply put it is the tendency of people to favor information that confirms their existing beliefs.

A student can look at their own progress and performance uncritically while complacently thinking:

> *Oh, I'm in the best school and training in the best style, so my techniques must be better than those other guys.*

Rather then viewing themselves and others with a *critical eye,* martial arts students can sometimes view others with criticism while viewing themselves with complacency.

This is not just a problem with junior students. Sometimes as students advance and have been in a school for some years, they get to the point where they only like to work at the things they are good at. Perhaps they only like to work with certain practice partners. Or perhaps they only show enthusiasm for certain aspects of the training. It is natural for martial arts students to have likes and preferences. What should be a concern to a martial arts teacher is when long term students stop making progress because they want the ego satisfaction of resting on their laurels.

As a matter of style, it is not appropriate for a martial arts teacher to be incessantly demanding and critical. There is a profound difference from *being critical* and having a *critical eye*. *Being critical* is a predisposition toward negativity and the arrogance to misinterpret it as a value. Having a *critical eye* is a matter of discernment. Acting upon that discernment is a matter of discretion. This is a distinction that martial arts teachers must know well.

It is important for a martial arts teacher to follow a process that:
1. *Recognizes learning blockages in the students.*
2. *Discerns the root cause of the blockages.*
3. *Takes corrective action.*
4. *Empowers the student with the tools to do this themselves.*

Other chapters in this book deal with the fundamental characteristic of vigilance as being important to both martial arts as a way of life and martial arts teaching. Certainly a martial arts teacher should be vigilant and constantly assessing the martial arts students' absorption and internalization of material.

It is likely that the martial arts teacher will need to reach outside of their martial art training to understand some of the factors that impede learning; for example the different types of bias mentioned earlier are not typically part of any martial arts teacher training curriculum.

Once the cause of the martial arts student's blockage is determined, the martial arts teacher can adjust the instruction to compensate for it. Sometimes, the martial arts teacher will decide not to make an adjustment. It may be that the martial arts student is distracted by something by some life event that is independent of martial arts. It may be that the martial arts teacher just decides to watch, wait, and re-evaluate. This is an entirely appropriate choice, if it is in fact a conscious decision.

Perhaps the biggest challenge and greatest reward is to help the martial arts students help themselves. One way of doing this is to help the martial arts students discover their style of learning. Different martial arts students need different things to make progress in their learning. Some student have an engineering mind and need logical, step-by-step, rationalized instruction. Other students have a holistic orientation and need a metaphorical interpretation of the material. Other students are kinesthetic learners and primarily learn by physically doing. Certainly there are other modes as well and some martial arts students need to learn by a combination of these styles.

The important thing is that the martial arts teacher knows what the appropriate learning style is for each martial arts student. Beyond that, the martial arts teacher needs to help the martial arts students to understand their own learning style, to that they can take more responsibility for their own progress. Ideally, martial arts teachers want to get their student to the point of self-awareness where they understand their own learning style and ask:

>Tell me...(engineer)
>Explain to me...(holistic)
>Show me...(kinesthetic)
>Etc...

Bad Mistakes Good Mistakes

In the early days of public education in the U.S., students of different levels were taught together in a one-room schoolhouse. By contrast, most public education today tracks students in homogenous cadres based on age and achievement. Other than home schooling or certain special situations the one-room school house is no longer a living part of the common American experience.

However, in martial arts, the one-room schoolhouse is an appropriate metaphor for the style of training that is typically done. While martial art schools often reserve some classes for beginners, children, or advanced students, most martial arts training occurs in classes with mixed levels of students of various ages and different levels of skill and achievement.

Even in recreational sports, it is common to separate participants by their capabilities (e.g., skill, size, gender, weight, etc.) into different classes.

So, in that regard, martial arts training presents some atypical challenges to both martial arts teachers and martial arts students. One of the most important challenges is to understand what happens when a class of martial arts students, with different levels of belt rank, are all practicing the same technique at the same time.

As was mentioned in other chapters of this book, martial arts techniques are practiced in a multi-dimensional learning context. Or to put it another way, each martial arts technique has multiple attributes or aspects related to its practice in a training situation. This not only applies to proper techniques, but also to more mundane activities, such as warm up and conditioning exercises.

These attributes can all be in play at the same time. However, the emphasis on these attributes can vary both according to the general capabilities of the martial arts student and according to the experience of the martial arts student with that particular technique.

Consider the following five attributes as being representative of the kind of quality dimensions that might be applied to the practice of a martial art technique in a training situation:

- **Gross Motions** – Here the martial arts students are just learning the kata/form of the technique, e.g. hand and foot positions, direction of movement. The focus here is on the basics of right and left, inside and outside, up and down, forward and backwards, etc.
- **Body Structure** – Next the martial arts students augment the basic movements of the technique with an awareness of the effect of those

159

movements on their body alignment. The martial arts students practice balance, good posture, and relaxation.

- **Precision** – In this aspect of the training, the martial arts students are refining the timing, speed, distance, power, and accuracy of their technique.
- **Focus** – Here martial arts students control their mind as they execute the technique. They keep external distraction out of their minds and they also do not fixate on any internal associations that may enter their minds. Even though the outcome of the practice technique is known in advance, the martial arts students learn not to let their minds jump to the last stage of the technique. Instead, the martial arts students learn to focus their mind, in a microsecond-by-microsecond fashion, on the appropriate parts of their body according to which stage of the technique they are in.
- **Advanced Martial Context** – It is likely that the martial arts teacher would have explained the tactical or situational objectives of the technique to the entire class when the technique was introduced. However, for an advanced student, even the practice of a technique in a solo kata requires more. The student should be able to relate the technique in focus to all of the techniques in that particular martial art style. That is, they should realize at what points in that technique they might morph it into a different technique. They should also develop an understanding of things like what situations may lead up to or follow the technique currently being practiced and how the technique same might relate to more advanced situations like multiple opponent attacks.

The following diagram symbolically represents these aspects as they might appear in the practice execution of a technique by martial arts students of different levels of skill. The dimensions are not to scale, but notice that all attributes are always present at each level of skill. They just become a bigger or smaller part of the practice as the martial arts student develops.

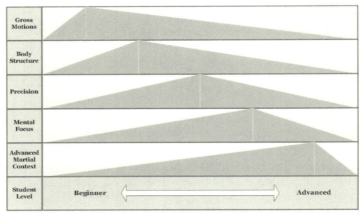

Figure 16: Sample Quality Attributes for Technique Practice

It may be apparent that in a martial arts class, the martial arts teacher will be looking for different things from different martial arts students, based on their level of proficiency. However, that expectation may not be apparent and needs to be explicitly communicated to the martial arts students.

The lower level martial arts students may be confused as to why some students are receiving certain corrections and others are not. They may be at a loss to explain to their family and friends support team why they are still practicing a particular technique or kata even though they supposedly learned it long ago. Also, a martial arts student, who is at the beginner level, may not even be aware of the concepts involved in the high levels of training and become confused as to why everyone is "doing the same thing." In contemporary American culture, it can be a good thing for martial arts teachers to take time to explain these things to their martial arts students, both for the martial arts students' own development and also to make them better and more articulate representatives of the martial arts.

Certainly, there are so many considerations in practicing even a basic technique that martial artists are always making mistakes. Even senior martial artists make mistakes. In Japanese martial arts, this is captured by the expression:

Even monkeys fall from trees.

In the U.S., where monkeys are not indigenous, it might be appropriate to change that to say:

Even squirrels fall from trees.

However, not all mistakes are equal. It is true that many mistakes in martial arts represent a potentially fatal outcome. However from a martial arts teaching perspective, it is important to understand that in martial arts training, some mistakes are appropriate to the martial arts students' level and some are not. Therefore there are *bad mistakes* and *good mistakes*.

When martial arts students make a mistake at something that they should have already mastered, that is a *bad mistake*. In American baseball, this might be referred to as a *rookie mistake*. That is a mistake which would be expected of a beginner; but is considered inappropriate for an experienced player. So in a martial arts class an experienced martial arts student and a junior martial arts student can be training side by side, do the exact same thing, and the martial arts teacher will admonish the senior student for carelessness while telling the junior student to just keep on doing what they are doing.

Good mistakes are when martial arts students begin to anticipate their next stage of training and find themselves making mistakes that the martial arts teacher would normally expect from a more senior martial arts student. This kind of mistake indicates that the martial arts student is absorbing the lesson material and is ready to progress.

Revelation and Concealment

From time to time martial artists will talk about *hidden techniques* or *secret techniques*. In earlier times, when martial arts had battlefield usefulness, these *trade secrets* of advanced martial arts practice were actually *military assets*. In modern times, information is much more accessible and there are fewer hidden techniques. In contemporary America, *hidden techniques* or *secret techniques* are more likely to be thought of as *intellectual capital* and their significance is more related to dojo marketing considerations, rather than a competitive edge related to life and death. As such they have more to do with the business model of a martial art school than they do with any mysterious martial initiation process.

Some martial arts teachers take a "show everything to anyone" approach. This is a generous style of teaching. The underlying concept is that the more the martial arts teacher gives, the more the martial arts student will want. Conversely, other martial arts teachers may selectively hold back their teaching so that the martial arts student must study over a protracted period of time in order to receive the full teaching. The idea is that martial arts students are motivated to reach the unseen goal on the other side of the mountain. There is nothing inherently wrong with these different approaches. They are representative of different business/teaching models that are based on different views of what motivates and retains martial arts students.

However, there is a more important contemporary consideration about *hidden techniques* or *secret techniques*. The important consideration is that there are some lessons a martial arts student can not learn until they are ready. Without the correct prior knowledge, the student will not have the background context to correctly learn the next lesson. Sometimes the reason for not showing a student a more advanced technique is because they will misapply it, perhaps even embarrassing the school or style. However, more often it is just a matter that the martial arts teacher knows precisely the immediately next step for the martial arts student's development and the martial arts teacher wants the student to focus their attention on that immediate next step.

From this perspective, the *secret* is not really a *secret*. It does not matter very much if the martial arts teacher takes a generous or stingy approach. The martial arts student simply requires the context acquired through practice and mastery of basics in order to understand more advanced lessons.

What is important is that the martial arts teacher understands the ability of each martial arts student to absorb information. Sometimes the martial arts teacher will reveal something that is clearly above a martial arts student's ability to understand, but not above a martial arts student's ability to wonder about or aspire to. This is like planting a seed in the martial arts student's mind. The martial arts teacher's intention is that the revelation will come back to the student in the future with a new sense of meaning, after the student has acquired a more advanced context as a result of more advanced training.

Every martial arts teacher understands that the martial arts have been around for a long time and that there are tremendous overlaps across different styles of martial arts. In the age of the internet, the notion of secret techniques is marginalized almost to the point of extinction. There are no martial arts secrets, just ignorant martial artists.

In our western European culture this idea is captured in the biblical notion of seeing vs. perceiving. In the Christian Gospel (Mark 8: 17-21), Jesus challenges his disciples' inability to not understand any but the most literal teaching:

> ...Do you still not see or understand? Are your hearts hardened?
> Do you have eyes but fail to see, and ears but fail to hear?...Do
> you still not understand?...

This distinction between observation and perception is a very important lesson for martial arts teachers. Many of the most important lessons in martial arts are hidden in plain sight. When novice martial arts students watch a technique demonstration, what do they see in their minds? Usually it is the finish - the impact of the hit, the throw, or the pin. So, when they go to copy or practice the technique, what happens? Their minds are fixated on the on the climax of the technique, the hit, or throw that characterizes the end of that move. Unfortunately, the end of a martial arts move is only the inescapable consequence of that which went before it.

This is analogous to an iceberg. 90% of the iceberg is below the surface, but a typical observer associates with only the 10% that they can easily see.

In the martial arts, the 90% that is not being perceived is right there in front of the student. If the technique climax is the 10%, then what is the 90% that is hidden in plain sight? It is qualities like distance, timing, balance, breathing, position, etc.

Martial arts training helps expose the complacent subjectivity of the everyday world. It is emotionally comforting to think that one has arrived, paid their dues, and has earned a place at the table. For example, consider these statements of accomplishment:

- I served in the army.
- I graduated from high school.
- I worked for that company for 40 years.
- I used to study Karate.
- I paid my taxes.

These are all good things. However, those sentences are all focused on some past accomplishments. The martial arts student needs to be able to focus in the present and not be distracted by the accomplishments of the past.

Furthermore, the martial arts student needs to see beyond superficial observations and detect the underlying dynamics of a martial situation.

The famous 19th century fencing teacher, Yamaoka Tesshu, was one of the last of the samurai. In the course of his life, he served in important posts for both the last feudal Shogun and for the parliamentary monarchy that replaced it. Master Tesshu was an accomplished individual who attained high levels of mastery in Zen, swordsmanship, and painting. Consider this lesson presented by Tesshu to his students:

> *One time, one of Master Tesshu's fencing students approached him and asked, "Master, what the essential element of our fencing style that sets it apart from other schools of swordsmanship." Master Tesshu replied, "I will not tell you that which should be apparent to you. Tomorrow, do not come to the fencing school. Instead, go to the local temple and pray continuously for the answer to your question. Do this every day. Do not return until you have seen the answer to your question."*
>
> *The next day, the student did exactly what Master Tesshu had specified. He went to the prescribed temple where he prayed and meditated all day. The student repeated this procedure day after day. After a week of intense effort, the student finally returned to the fencing school. Upon seeing Master Tesshu, the student reported, "I went to the temple every day and prayed intensively all day long. Even so, no inspiration came to me. Then, yesterday as I was leaving the temple, I noticed the inscription above the shrine. It said: 'The Gift of Fearlessness.' Was that what you meant?"*
>
> *"Exactly!" replied Master Tesshu. "That is the secret of our fencing style. However, it is important that you understand this fully. In other fencing schools, some warriors are not afraid to face enemies who are armed with swords. Yet these same warriors are afraid to face their own passions and delusions. In our way of fencing, we are never afraid to face either our external enemies or our own inner enemies."*

The Sword of No-Sword : Life of the Master Warrior Tesshu. John Stevens

Tesshu's student was asking for something that he needed to find out for himself. Yet Tesshu knew how to direct that student so that he could find the "concealed" truth. This is a model for all martial arts teachers.

Belief vs. Trust

> **Believe:**
> - *to have a firm religious faith*
> - *to accept something as true, genuine, or real*
>
> **Trust:**
> - *assured reliance on the character, ability, strength, or truth of someone or something*
> - *one in which confidence is placed*

Merriam-Webster Dictionary

Martial arts have a number of parallels with religions. Martial art styles are analogous to denominations, the martial art school's membership is analogous to a congregation, and the martial art training hall is analogous to the house of worship. Both religion and martial arts have traditions, rules, and hierarchies. Both have an ethos of self-betterment through following a disciplined approach to life. There are even some common practices, such as meditation, which can be found, in some form, in both religion and martial arts.

In earlier tribal cultures, the connection between religion and warrior societies was much closer than in contemporary America. Tribal cultures have tighter integration across the multiple aspects of a person's life. For example, coming of age preparation in tribal societies may involve both induction into a warrior society and also taking on some ceremonial and religious responsibilities as an adult in the community.

Even in larger non-tribal societies there have, in earlier times, been strong crossover connections between religions and martial arts. For example, the name of the old Shinto-Style sword schools refers to "the way of the gods" and reflects the ancient Japanese tradition that the school's founder learned the techniques of sword fighting from mythological demi-gods. In western culture, we have our own similar traditions and legendary examples of connections between supernatural power and martial power. King Arthur, Beowulf, Thor, Achilles, Moses, Joshua, Gideon and other figures possessed martial powers associated with supernatural forces tied to their religious contexts. Back in the middle ages there were many examples of religion and martial training mixing. Consider the Christian crusaders (e.g., the orders of Templar Knights Hospitaller, Teutonic Knights), their Islamic opponents (e.g., Janissaries, Assassins), or the Buddhist warrior monks of feudal Japan. After the middle ages, the Reformation in Europe saw a mix of politics, religion, and warfare which lasted to some degree up through the Enlightenment and the founding of the United States. However, between the Middle Ages and the

Enlightenment warfare began to change through the introduction of firearms. So while there was still a strong dynamic between religion, politics, and war, there was no longer the need to focus on individual martial achievement through pursuit of martial arts.

Religion and martial arts eventually separated in modern culture. However, the legacy of the past can still be seen in some cultural contexts. For example, in contemporary Christian iconography Saint George and Saint Michael are normally identifiable by martial imagery involving their holding weapons. Traces of the legacy can also be found in musical lyrics from religious hymns like *Onward Christian Soldiers* to patriotic songs like *The Battle Hymn of the Republic*.

While those cultural references still exist as indicators of American history and basic human proclivity, the fact remains that in contemporary America, martial arts are essentially secular. There are certainly examples where a martial arts school may be co-located in a building which is also used for religious purposes. In such cases the religious organizations are typically providing a venue as a public service just as they might for an aerobics class, a cultural event, or a community organization. There are also some martial art instructors who might be religiously inclined and see their martial arts teaching as a ministerial calling. That is merely their personal point of view. It does not make their martial art a religion, even if they occasionally use religiously based terminology to help explain their teaching points or are able to use martial arts to reinforce moral or ethical principles.

At the most basic level what makes martial arts different from religions in contemporary America is that martial arts are secular pursuits. There is no deity in the martial arts school. The architectural layout of a martial art school may have characteristics that were derived from the design of temples, but that is just the modern reflection of an artifact of cultural heritage. Actions that would have the intent of worship in a religion have analogs in martial arts, but the intent is very different. For example, bowing might be an act of worship in some religions. However, in martial arts bowing is simply a sign of martial respect (akin to a military salute).

Meditation, which might be practiced as a form of prayer in a religion, has a completely different context in martial arts. In martial arts meditation is employed as a method of mental discipline to clear away stray thoughts and train the mind not to wander. The use of oriental words like *ki* or *chi* to describe abstract concepts related to inner power is simply shorthand terminology to align students to a level of concentration where they can establish the proper state of mind to practice effectively to the point at which the utility of the whole begins to exceed the sum of the parts.

It is important that martial arts teachers understand the historical connections between religion and martial arts and can articulate the modern interpretation of these relationships to their students. Martial arts teachers are transmitting a universal and secular value-based systems to their students. So it is important for both martial arts teachers and students to understand that as individuals they have a personal process for incorporating and reconciling martial arts values with other value systems that martial arts teachers and students participate in.

Part of the role of a martial arts teacher is not only to transmit knowledge, but also to encourage and inspire growth. In this regard, the martial arts teacher attempts to encourage the student to embrace and aspire towards a set of goals along a path that the student has not traveled previously. Here again there are analogous, but differing, approaches used in religions and martial arts.

For the purpose of this discussion the terms *belief* and *trust* will be used. In their dictionary definition and common usage, these two terms have overlapping meanings. However, for the purposes of this discussion, the more subtle uniqueness of each term will be emphasized to illustrate a point.

In religious practice there is the concept of *belief* is to create a mental bridge for the practitioner, in order to help them connect from where they are in the present to their future state of fulfillment. To *believe* something is to accept it as true, even if it is beyond human ability to understand. In religion, *belief* has a central role because many theological concepts describe things that are inherently beyond human experience. In the context of religion, the concept of *belief* is often associated with the related concept of *faith*. In many western religious traditions, this ability to accept religious constructs as true is a result of the divine gift of *faith*.

There is an old saying about religion:

> *For those who don't believe, no proof is sufficient.*
> *For those who believe, no proof is necessary.*

In the context of religion, *belief* is more a matter of *faith* - not because it deals with abstractions, but because those abstractions apply to subjects that are inherently beyond human experience.

Martial arts teachers are also trying to help students bridge their thinking from their current state to some future state. However, instead of encouraging by fostering *belief*, it is more appropriate for martial arts teachers to employ the concept of *trust*. As opposed to *belief*, trust is more a matter of building a set of layered expectations overtime.

Consider a person preparing for a very long, cross-country road trip in their car, through isolated areas with rough terrain. Hopefully the person is aware of the risks and is confident that they will not have a breakdown along the way. In the context of this discussion the person might say:

> *I feel confident going on this trip because in the advertisements, my brand and model of car is always depicted as being reliable.*

This is an example of a person who *believes* things will go well and is acting on faith. Whereas, a statement like...

> *I feel confident going on this trip because I have checked the tires and fluid levels in the car and I have an emergency kit in my trunk.*

This is an example of *trust*.

Take another comparison. A music fan may *believe* that their favorite band is the best in the world. However, a jazz quartet soloist must *trust* in the musical ability of the piano player, bass guitarist and drummer.

Finally, consider an NFL team. A fan watching on television may *believe* in the efficacy of his team's in the offensive line; the quarterback actually needs to *trust* the efficacy of his team's offensive line.

The misapplication of *belief* to a secular situation is sometimes referred to as a *leap of faith*. This can be the cause of problems. A parent who is confronted because of some problem caused by their child may refuse to *believe* that their child could have done something wrong. However, a parent who decides to *trust* their child has made a measured calculation of the child's capabilities and age specific reliability for a particular situation. That parent *trusts* their child to do A, B, & C, given the specific circumstances of X, Y, & Z.

In daily secular lives, *belief* can be a shortcut for *trust*. When people are too busy, or too lazy, to inspect and assess situations, then *belief* might sometimes be substituted for *trust*. When a person does this they are sometimes referred to as being naïve. By this definition, it is not a matter of being too *trusting*, rather it is a matter of *believing* rather than *trusting*. One of the problems with the misapplication of *belief* in secular matters is that belief can be delusional; it is easier to *believe* a simpler story then to go through the effort of sorting out a more complex story. People like to *believe* things that make their lives easier to understand. This takes much less effort than to understand many different things and applying *trust*.

Trust is a key element of martial arts practice. In martial arts training, practitioners *trust* each other with their lives. Martial artists *trust* their technique, both to keep their partner safe in practice and to keep themselves save in a conflict situation. The martial arts student *trusts* the martial arts teacher to provide a safe training environment and to provide the appropriate guidance and instruction. Martial artists in general and martial arts teachers specifically must be *trustworthy*. Otherwise martial arts training and teaching have no foundation for commitment. This applies both to the commitment to spend long hours in hard training and also the commitment to face an opponent and apply a technique as if one's life depends on it. When helping a martial arts student to learn a difficult technique, a martial arts teacher will want the student to visualize the result. Sometimes the martial arts teacher might tell the student:

Believe that you can do it!

However, this is not quite correct. It is more appropriate to express it as:

Trust in the efficacy of the technique and commit to your execution of it.

In martial arts, *trust* as opposed to *belief*, does not turn off critical thinking, it simply contextualizes it.

For purposes of this discussion it is not so important that these terms can have different contextual uses. What is important is to understand that there is a need for martial arts teachers to help students bridge their thinking from where they are to where they should be and that there are different ways of thinking about how to foster this future vision. In this discussion, the terms *belief* and *trust* have been narrowly defined to accentuate the difference between two approaches to establish a visualization bridge. One of the approaches is recommended as being the more appropriate one for martial arts instructors to follow. The following table summarizes the attributes distinguishing these two approaches as discussed in this chapter.

Characteristic	Term	
	Belief	**Trust**
Acquisition	Earned	Gifted and Accepted
Internalization	Quantum	Incremental
Involvement	Bystander	Participant
Scope	Unconditional	Conditional

Table 9 : Contrasting Belief v.s. Trust

The reason that the distinction is being made between the two approaches is that there is a difference between teaching and learning abstract concepts that are beyond human experience and those that are simply beyond an individual's personal experience.

The famous sword master, Miyamoto Musashi summed this up well in the conclusion to his <u>Book of Five Rings</u> where he cautions students about thinking that everything beyond their personal experience and comprehension is also beyond human experience and comprehension.

...What is called the spirit of the void is where there is nothing. It is not included in man's knowledge. Of course the void is nothingness. By knowing things that exist, you can know that which does not exist. That is the void. When people in this world look at things mistakenly, and think that what they do not understand must be the void. This is not the true void. It is simply bewilderment...

Martial arts teachers are responsible for establishing the atmosphere of *trust* in their schools. That *trust* is the basis for self-exploration and discovery. Without that basis of trust, it is difficult for students to confront their habits of complacency and rid themselves of the bewilderment that Musashi was referring to.

The Bigger Context

In the middle of the 17 century C.E. Musashi, retired to reflect on his career as a martial artist and compose his thoughts in his classic essay, <u>The Book of Five Rings</u>.

While Musashi was commenting on the characteristics of the life of a samurai warrior, his observations were more specifically focused on how the warrior's life was shaped by the dedicated pursuit of the martial art of fencing. As a result, only a little extrapolation is required to apply Musashi's observations to contemporary martial artists.

In Musashi's time, people did not have careers or avocations as we know them today. Instead, most people were born into a class or cast which predetermined how they would live their lives. For example, military service was not a job, an enlistment, or a career; it was an inherited way of life, extending from childhood to old age. The same principle applied to other occupations such as farming or craft trades. Likewise, those warriors who dedicated themselves to the advanced study of martial arts were not merely engaged in a hobby or pastime. Rather, they were consecrating themselves to a way of life which further defined their dress, their place in society, their thinking and their actions.

In the first chapter of *The Book of Five Rings*, Musashi briefly highlights the main points defining martial arts as they existed back then:

- **Martial arts present only one possible life path:** There are many other virtuous disciplines to which a person can devote their life. Some examples include: religion, public service, health care, academics, fine arts, martial arts, etc.

- **Martial arts are not just a physical pursuit:** They are a way of life. Training the mind and understanding the wider world is as important as physical training.

- **Even without native talent, dedication and hard work in both physical training and improving one's mind will lead to progress and competency in martial arts:** However, few practitioners penetrate to the deepest levels of martial arts understanding.

- **The martial artist way of life is unique in that it requires a constant and resolute acceptance of death:** People from other pursuits might from time-to-time be virtuous to the point of death (e.g., martyrdom of a religious person, heroic death in the pursuit of duty, courage in the face of terminal illness, etc.) However, the

172

martial artist way of life is different because of its focus on dealing with violent struggles between individuals.

Musashi's views on this subject may have been hard-earned by virtue of his life of training, study, and fighting. However, they were not unique or unusually insightful. Musashi's point of view was very consistent with the thinking of other martial arts commentators of his day.

From a contemporary perspective, Musashi's views are still valid. However, in contemporary American culture, we have a very different world view. So there is value in reexamining his ideas from a modern perspective. Even today, Musashi's four points resound as the backdrop for contemporary martial arts training.

It is the role of the martial arts teacher to confront the martial arts students with the bigger context of martial arts. This bigger context includes the relationships of martial arts students and society as a whole. It also includes the role of martial arts training within the martial arts students' individual lives. Whether or not the martial arts students choose to resonate with message is up to them. However, the martial arts teachers' role is to provide the martial arts students with the spark to light their way.

One Technique

In many human endeavors, there is an underlying search for a unifying principle. Manifestations of this striving can be seen in art, religion, philosophy, and science.

In the martial arts, this is frequently depicted by the Taoist symbol called the *Taijitu* or the *Yin-Yang symbol*. The symbol implies the existence of two opposing forces. One force is called Yin and is represented by the black; the other force is called Yang and is represented by the white. The line separating them is curved so that the Yin and Yang forces appear to flow into each other. This represents harmony. Both sides of the symbol have a dot of the opposite color in them. The dots represent the notion that in nature Yin and Yang never exist in their pure state and they are really both manifestations of the same reality.

Figure 17: Taijitu Symbol

When used in the context of the martial arts, the Taijitu symbol represents martial arts training as a process for harmonizing and unifying opposites such as hardness and softness, motion and stillness, etc.

Consider martial arts students when they are first learning to use a weapon. A novice student will move the weapon with uncoordinated force. There are many reasons for this. One reason for this is that the eye of the novice student can only track the gross movements of the weapon and key factors like weight shifting and center of balance initially go unrecognized. Another reason is that maintaining the spirit of commitment while reserving the physical initiation of a committed movement is beyond the perception of a beginner. In any event, the overuse of strength to wield a weapon may be sufficient to succeed in a conflict with a less skilled opponent, but it is not truly martial arts. Over time and with practice, martial arts students learn the characteristics (i.e., weight, balance, length, flexibility, etc.) of the weapon and begin to adjust their body motions to adapt to the specific characteristics of the weapon. It can be said that martial arts students' progress takes them from trying to enforce the weapon to do what they want to allowing the characteristics of the weapon to manifest themselves through the advanced students' movements.

In martial arts this would be called "being one with the weapon". Naturally this principle exists in endeavors outside of martial arts. Golf, tennis, baseball, hockey, lacrosse, basketball, and many other activities share the need to work with equipment. However, in most situations, those activities are practiced recreationally, i.e. *for fun*, rather than *for self improvement*. As a result, many of those sports practitioners do not get to the higher level of practice that is sometimes referred to as the *inner game*. Also, while sports practice can be quite competitive, martial arts are unique in that their practice is focused on the simulation of saving and taking lives. As a result, the need to move toward that state of oneness has more pressing urgency.

In martial arts, there is an expression borrowed from Zen Buddhism that describes one aspect of the martial art principle of unity.

Beginners mind – Master's mind

The idea is that in some way a master has come around full circle to the beginning. Sometimes people do not quite understand this saying and wonder that if the master is back at the same place, what was the purpose of the journey? Metaphorically, it can be explained better if one visualizes the analogy in three dimensions rather than two. In two dimensions, an observer might witness a journey that appears to go in a circle. From the perspective of three dimensions, that same journey might reveal itself to be a spiral as in a person traveling up a mountain. Looking from above or below, the journey appears to be a circle returning to the same spot. However, when looking from the side, it is apparent that the person has reached a higher elevation by completing a spiral path.

One reason that the beginner and master have something of the same mind is because of the pedagogy (i.e., forms, traditions teachings, customs, etc.) of their martial arts style. When beginners walk into a martial arts school for the first time, they know nothing of this. Over much time and practice, the martial arts student is no longer a beginner and has become engrossed with the pedagogy of that martial arts style. At this point, the martial arts student is inevitably looking at the pointing hand, not the moon.

Eventually, some martial arts students can reach a point of mastery where they can begin to transcend the pedagogy of their style. So in that sense, their master's mind is like their beginner's mind in that it is free of the forms imposed by the pedagogy. While it is possible for some masters to transcend the pedagogy of their style, this does not diminish the value of the forms, traditions teachings, customs, etc. These artifacts are, in fact, valuable blessings. They are the tools by which the transformation of the martial artist is accomplished. However, they are not the ultimate goal.

As martial arts teachers go about mastering and communicating the syllabus of their martial arts style, they should progressively see more connection across the different techniques and variations of those techniques. In fact, as times goes on, they will even see those connections between their own martial arts style and others.

As martial arts teachers progress, their teaching should become richer. Even if their syllabus is unchanged, their teaching matures. While a novice martial arts teacher may correctly teach a technique, a more advanced martial arts teacher can, provided the level of the martial arts student is correct, teach the relationships between techniques.

Eventually, the martial arts master teachers begin to view all of the techniques within the syllabus of their style as being related. In an abstract sense, they become unified into one logical technique.

In western thought, this perspective on the concept of oneness as an advanced teaching is captured in similar Jewish and Christian stories.

According to tradition, a skeptic once sought to annoy the Jewish philosopher Hillel (110B.C.E. - 7C.E.). Knowing already that Jewish law contained over 600 biblical ordinances plus accompanying case law, commentaries, traditional practices, and social conventions related to compliance, the skeptic challenged Hillel to teach him the entirety of Jewish law in the amount of time that Hillel could balance himself on one foot. Without hesitation, Hillel accepted the challenge and pronounced:

> *That which is hateful to you, do not do to your neighbor. That is the whole Torah; the rest is commentary. Go and study it.*

A century later, Christian tradition (Matthew 22: 34-40) has Jesus responding in a similar way when an "expert" in Jewish law (who evidently had not studied Hillel) provocatively asked Jesus:

> *Teacher, which is the greatest commandment in the Law (Torah)?*

Jesus' famous reply was;

> *Love the Lord your God with all your heart and with all your soul and with your entire mind. This is the first and greatest commandment. And the second is like it: Love your neighbor as yourself. All of the law and the prophets derive from these two commandments.*

The challenge for martial arts teachers is similar. Instead of biblical ordinances, they have their style's syllabus. It is the responsibility of a martial arts teacher to personally struggle to find the unity from which the diversity of techniques and training methods derive.

About the Cover

Hotei Pointing at the Moon

Clockwise from the top left:

- Sengai Gibon, Japanese, 1750-1837
- Fugai Ekun, Japanese, 1568–1654
- Hakuin Ekaku, Japanese, 1685-1768

In Zen Buddhist art, the act of pointing at the moon is a classic theme for paintings. This subject is used as a metaphor for both self-realization and the limitations inherent in teaching.

The story's origin is a parable told by Buddha to his young cousin, Ananda, as part of the Surangama (i.e. *indestructible*) Sutra. However, in Zen painting, the figure doing the pointing is often represented as the semi-mythical monk Hotei. Hotei is a mendicant; always traveling and begging for each meal. Although he eats only little and has no possessions, Hotei is jokingly depicted with a big belly and a large sack as symbols for his fullness of spirit. In Zen Buddhist art, Hotei is often chosen as an observer of natural phenomena. In this classic painting theme, Hotei is our guide and teacher. Hotei's pointing introduces us to our subject, the moon.

Hotei's raised finger can be understood to represent the canonical body of knowledge and practice that leads to the truth. The moon represents the more abstract attainment which inherently transcends that canon. For many Buddhists, that canon is the Dharma. For many Christians it is the Bible. For martial artists, the teachings and traditions of their style and school are that canon of knowledge.

Since the ultimate attainment is hidden in plain sight, the pointing is necessary. We might not otherwise take time to truly notice the moon unless it was explicitly called out to us.

However, at another level, the ultimate represented by the moon is also irrelevant. The goal, no matter how bright and clear, is always distant. Only the acts of pointing, following the point, and looking toward the ultimate are existentially significant. Hence, two of the three artists did not think it important enough to even include the moon in their paintings. Their artistic interpretations focus totally on the journey, not the destination.

The inscription in the second painting reads:

> *His life is not poor*
> *He has riches beyond measure*
> *Pointing to the moon, gazing at the moon*
> *This old guest follows the way*

177